HOW TO STOP BEING A COMPULSIVE LIAR

The Complete Guide to Stop Pathological Lying and Start Living an Honest Life

JAMIE WILLIAMS

OAKRIDGE PRESS

PREFACE

What would it feel like to see yourself through the eyes of those you care about? I saw how Jack felt when his wife, Alvine, talked about his compulsive lying. Alvine loved her husband but had serious concerns about their relationship because of his habitual lies. During one of our coaching sessions, she said everything was just so confusing around him. In her words, "It's so confusing that I often doubt if I really know him."

Eric had similar concerns about the behavior of his wife, Eva. He said that she lied about trivial and very obvious things. These were his exact words, "I sometimes doubt myself and query my experiences because of her lies. She makes me feel like a paranoid wreck whenever I ask if she's telling me the truth."

I could tell that both Jack and Eva were unhappy about the effects of their condition on those around them. Further, it was obvious that they felt trapped: They were genuinely perplexed and wanted a way out of their predicament, but they didn't know how. I remember during my session with Jack and Alvine, Jack said he wished there was a reset button in his brain that someone could press to make him stop lying.

Where It All Started

Jack's wish for a reset button hit a deep spot in my heart. That was the day I realized how much I hate to see anyone feel trapped or helpless. That passion has led to years of research, studying, consultations, and professional experience that culminated in writing this book.

Many people dismiss pathological lying (or compulsive lying) as an excuse for bad behavior. They do not realize that lying can be addictive and become a challenge for pathological liars to avoid. Invariably, they fail to understand that pathological liars need help and support rather than condemnation.

In my professional practice as a life coach, I have had the privilege to help several clients manage and conquer their challenges with compulsive lying and better the relationships in their lives. This book contains insights from those experiences, my formal education as a psychologist, and years of extensive research on compulsive lying.

What to Expect

If you are trying to overcome the habit of lying, you are not alone. There are several other people out there like you. Moreover, help is available for you. Each page of this book contains credible and practicable information that will teach you effective strategies for living a more honest life. That would, in turn, help you ensure better and long-lasting relationships.

You will find useful information, backed with real-life stories, on how to practice honesty in your daily life despite your struggles. The advice and strategies in this book have worked for several people, and they will work for you too as you strive for a life of honesty.

Start Now!

The journey toward becoming an honest person is neither short nor easy, but you must start from somewhere. Reading this book is indeed a good place to start. Keep reading to get the help that you need, and start taking bold steps toward your victory over compulsive lying.

1

THE CONCEPT OF LYING

8

Honesty is perhaps the greatest moral dilemma for humans. We all try to hide or ignore the truth, but doing that does not always count as lying. For instance, when someone asks you, "how are you?" do you honestly tell them what's going on in your life? You say, "Fine" regardless of how you feel at the time.

As far as you are concerned, they are just exchanging pleasantries with you, so you ignore the truth about how you feel and tell them that you're okay. Does that mean you lied? Certainly not.

How about when you wear makeup? People look at you in admiration and wonder how you manage to stay young. Do you tell all your admirers that you don't look that good without makeup? When someone compliments your smooth face, you appreciate them and hide the truth from them. Does that also count as a lie? Most people will say no, it doesn't.

It is, therefore, clear that lying is not just about hiding or ignoring the truth. So then, let us explore the concept of lying by first defining what it is.

What Is Lying?

Lying is intentionally communicating something that you know to be untrue when those you are communicating with expect and believe that you are being honest. It is conveying a message that you don't believe with the motive to deceive or mislead someone else to accept it as the truth.

According to the above definition, you lie when the following things happen:

- You verbally or nonverbally convey a false message.
- You know and believe that the message you are conveying is false.
- Your motive is to make the receiver(s) of your false message accept it as true.
- Your recipients expect and assume that you are being honest.

That means you have not lied if you convey a false message thinking it is true. For instance, many years ago, people believed that the earth was flat, and that was what they told their children. That information was false, but it was not a lie since those who said it also believed it. Conversely, if I tell you now that the earth is spherical when I actually believe that it is flat, I am telling you a lie. In truth, the earth is spherical, but my motive to deceive you into believing it when I think it's false makes it a lie.

The expectations of people also matter in defining lies. Have you ever attended a comedy show? Many comedians cook up funny stories while cracking jokes. However, most people don't attend comedy shows expecting the comedians to be honest. They expect the comedians to be funny and know that most of the funny stories they will hear probably never happened.

You can't say then, that comedians lie while cracking jokes. They make stories up quite often, but that does not make them habitual liars. Their stories are not lies because their motive was not to deceive anybody. Moreover, even their recipients don't expect true-life stories from them.

These thoughts about lying are from ancient philosophies. We will examine these fundamental philosophies to better understand the concept of lying.

Philosophies Surrounding Lying

There are two main philosophical traditions about lying. One of those traditions traces back to Aristotle, who opined that lying is never justified, no matter the circumstance. The other came from Plato, who made excuses for lying in some situations.

Many philosophers have built ideologies on these two fundamental philosophies. For instance, moral absolutists like Kant, Aquinas, and Augustine drew heavily from Aristotle's school of thought about lying. However, Aristotle himself did not advocate radical honesty. He permitted magnanimous people to tell self-deprecating lies.

Aristotle on Self-Deprecating Lies

A self-deprecating lie is one you tell to belittle yourself or your efforts. For instance, imagine that you prepared thoroughly for an exam and scored 100% when you wrote it. People began to congratulate you, marvel at your intelligence, and commend your hard work. In response, you told them that you didn't study that much; you were only lucky to have that score. Well, you told them a lie, albeit self-deprecating.

According to Aristotle, such lies humble you and will not hurt anyone. They are, therefore, permissible since they are lies with pure and noble intentions.

Plato's Two Types of Lies

Plato's philosophy is more liberal than Aristotle's. It leaves more room for justifiable lies beyond self-deprecation.

Plato said there are two types of lies: true falsehoods and verbal falsehoods. True falsehood is the lie you tell when being honest is the right thing to do. Pluto said such lies are neither justifiable nor proper under any circumstance. On the other hand, verbal falsehood is the lies you tell when being honest is the wrong thing to do. According to Pluto, these include lying against your enemies, cooking up stories to establish a valid point, or lying to keep or protect a friend from danger.

If someone walks up to you to ask for your friend's whereabouts, and you know they intend to harm your friend, would it be wrong to lie that you don't know their whereabouts? Plato categorized these lies as vocal falsehoods and opined that they were morally justifiable. His teacher, Socrates, believed and taught his students that a good friend tells verbal lies to protect their friends.

Ancient Philosophies vs. Modern Thoughts

These two philosophical traditions about lying have found their way into the modern-day concept of lying. However, people are no longer familiar with terms like verbal falsehood and true falsehood. We now describe lies as black lies, white lies, big lies, blue lies, and so on. It is vital to understand these modern-day classifications as we further explore the concept of lying.

Modern-Day Classification of Lies

Every lie is with the intent to deceive, but all lies are not the same. A white lie is one that you tell for a good cause. On the other hand, a black lie is one that you tell for a bad cause. A blue lie has both good and bad reasons. Frequent lies for no particular reason could be compulsive lies.

White Lies

Imagine that an overweight friend starts going to the gym to lose weight. One week after starting, they ask you if they are already losing weight. How would you respond?

To say the truth, one week is too short to start seeing noticeable results. However, telling them the truth may hurt their feelings and discourage them from continuing their weight loss journey. You can, therefore, lie that you see the results already. Your intention for telling such a lie is good, so it is a white lie.

White lies have a close link with empathy and emotional intelligence. You will occasionally tell white lies if you are sensitive to how people feel.

Black Lies

Black lies have deliberate, evil intentions. They are often told for selfish gain, not minding that the lie will hurt someone else. An example of a black lie is telling lies against somebody you dislike to make other people dislike them.

Blue Lies

Blue lies have both good and bad intentions, which makes them somewhat complicated to define from moral and ethical perspectives. They are often for the benefit of a community or group, although they may hurt some people. Politicians and public officers, like policemen, often tell these kinds of lies.

A politician speaking during a campaign may say, "If you vote for that other party, they will destroy this country." He knows that statement is not true, but in his mind, he's lying in the interest of his party and for the sake of the country. He sincerely believes that his party will govern the country better, so he tells a blue lie to convince people to vote for them.

Compulsive Lie

Compulsive lies belong to a separate category because there is usually no good or bad intention behind them. They are often a result of self-esteem issues or psychological disorders. People who tell compulsive lies would lie even when saying the truth is the easier option. They need therapeutic help.

The Effects of Lies

It is easier to lie when you don't know how your lies affect the people who receive the misinformation. If they find out you lied to them, they will find it hard to keep trusting you. Over time, and with more lies, they begin to second-guess everything you say, and your relationship with them will not remain the same.

Think about why people lose faith in the government or political system. Lies and failed promises would top the list. All politicians are suspected of lying because others before them did. That is what happens when people are lied to or deceived repeatedly; they develop trust issues and start suspecting even innocent people.

Lies also affect empathy. You may find it hard to help people if someone lied to get help from you in the past. That means whenever you lie to a person, you risk damaging the person's trust and empathy. These can, in turn, make life more difficult for other people and make the world a worse place.

Other effects of lying on the receiver include:
- feeling disrespected by the person who lied
- feeling like a fool for believing the lie

Despite all of these effects, people still lie. So, what are the reasons or motivations behind lying? Why does the average person still tell one to two lies daily?

Why People Lie

Research shows that most people are not radically honest. The average person makes an excuse for white lies and may tell black and blue lies once in a while too. These account for the one to two lies that the average person tells daily.

Here are the common reasons why people lie.

To Avoid Consequences

People lie to cover their mistakes and avoid the consequences. Some of these are honest mistakes while others are intentional misdeeds. For instance, a child broke a plate and lied that they didn't know about the broken plate. They lied to avoid consequences.

For Personal Profit or Gain

People lie to obtain rewards or for other forms of personal gain. Sometimes they deserve the reward, but it may not be readily obtainable without the lie. Lying about work experience to increase your chances during a work interview falls in this category.

To Win Admiration or Favor

People lie to give themselves a good image or create a positive impression. These could be little white lies, small exaggerations, or bogus lies.

To Escape Awkward Situations

Imagine that you are on a long phone call and don't know how to end the call. You may claim that you have a visitor at the door. Such a lie was for no mischievous reason. You were only trying to escape an awkward situation.

Other reasons why people lie include:

- for protection (themselves or someone else)
- a means of avoiding embarrassment
- to gain power or control over people

Lying Creates a Vicious Cycle

Research shows that each lie causes brain changes that make it easier to tell another lie. The liar feels smarter with each lie and tends to tell more lies to cover up previous lies. These can create a vicious cycle where they form a habit of lying. They end up with a tangled web of lies and dread being caught or exposed.

Liars often go to any length to sell a lie as the truth. They often respond in the following ways when they are exposed or confronted.

- Pass the blame to someone else.
- Get angry that you found the truth and accuse you of snooping.
- Become defensive.
- Blame you for overreacting or taking their statements out of context.
- Out rightly deny the lie.
- Attempt to gaslight the victim.
- Make excuses for their lies or try to explain them away.

Despite being caught, most habitual liars will still lie again. It is even more challenging for pathological liars because they can't help but lie.

Can't Help but Lie

Pathological liars (also called compulsive liars) can't help but lie. It would be helpful to clarify that while most people use the two terms interchangeably, some people argue that they are different. The medical literature, however, agrees that these terms mean the same thing. I agree with the conventional medical definition that these two terms are interchangeable. However, I wish to highlight the differences some believe those terms have.

Some mental health professionals define compulsive lying as an uncontrollable habit of telling lies without an ulterior motive. According to that framework, compulsive liars may tell lies that negatively affect their image or damage their reputation.

Pathological liars, on the other hand, often have a clear motive for lying. They may lie to gain admiration, pity, help, or attention. Moreover, pathological liars sometimes add elements of truth to their lies to make them more credible. They lie to get internal gratification even when the lie seems to be self-harming.

Symptoms of a Pathological Liar

• They use lies as a coping mechanism for internal deficiencies. For instance, some pathological liars lie to cope with the effects of abuse or childhood trauma. Some pathological liars suffer from a mental health illness or have a genetic condition that predisposes them.

• Pathological liars are goal-oriented. While they have little awareness of the lies they tell, their goal for lying is usually clear. They want to manipulate people, have their way, or get validation.

• Pathological liars disregard the feelings and rights of the people they lie to. It is, therefore, difficult for them to realize how much they hurt the people they love with their lies.

• People often describe pathological liars as cunning or manipulative. They almost always have their way by hook or by crook.

• Pathological liars know how to create impressive stories that they either treat or maintain over time. They usually end up believing their lies and lose their grip on reality.

• It is easier to catch a compulsive liar than a pathological liar. Pathological liars master the art of lying through their persistent lies. They become so excellent that it becomes extremely difficult to spot their lies.

• Pathological liars exude lots of confidence while lying. As such, the usual verbal and nonverbal cues for spotting lies may be absent while they are lying. For instance, while the average liar cannot maintain eye contact while lying, a pathological liar may look straight into your eyes and lie to you without batting an eyelid.

• Confronting a pathological liar never makes them remorseful. They become defensive and hostile in the face of confrontation. Moreover, they rarely admit their dishonesty.

• Pathological liars do not value truth. As such, lying is more comfortable for them than telling the truth.

Symptoms of a Compulsive Liar

- Nothing is too small or too serious for a compulsive liar to lie about. Lying often feels like the right thing to do. Moreover, they find honesty and truthfulness very awkward.

- Compulsive lying usually starts in childhood, while pathological lying often develops during the teenage years.

- The environment plays a pivotal role in the making of a compulsive liar. Most compulsive liars grew up where lying was routinely used as a survival tool.

- Compulsive liars usually avoid confrontations when the truth comes out. They feel ashamed when they are caught.

- Mental health illnesses have no direct link with compulsive lying. It is, however, more common in people with bipolar disorder, borderline personality disorder, and attention deficit hyperactivity disorder.

- People don't see compulsive liars as overly cunning or manipulative people. They just have a bad habit that they find difficult to break. This bad habit, however, negatively affects vital relationships in their lives.

- Compulsive liars are not so sophisticated, so they are easier to catch than pathological liars. When they tell elaborate stories, the pieces usually don't add up. Conversely, pathological liars can build one lie upon another, and everything would make perfect sense.

- People who know how to read body language can easily spot a compulsive liar. They exhibit typical lying behaviors, including excessive sweating, rambling, or avoiding direct eye contact.

- Compulsive liars lie spontaneously without thinking much about what they would say. Most times, they build their lies around what people prefer to hear. No clear personal benefits are attached to their lies.

- Compulsive liars still have a firm grip on reality. They don't believe their lies and can still differentiate between lies and reality.

- Compulsive liars are more prone to admitting their wrongdoing than pathological liars. That might, however, not prevent them from lying again.

Whichever way we look at it, both compulsive and pathological lying are conditions that make it difficult for people who suffer from it not to tell lies. Pathological liars can, however, eventually stop lying when they get appropriate help.

Different research studies have tried to evaluate the prevalence of pathological lying. The reports say that eight to thirteen percent of the world population are pathological liars (Curtis & Hart, 2020). Research also shows that while children start lying anywhere from age three to eight, pathological lying usually begins during the teenage years, with an average onset age of 16 (BetterHelp Editorial Team, 2022). There are no differences when it comes to race, gender, and geographic location.

Characteristic Traits of Pathological/Compulsive Lying

As we have seen, people lie for several reasons. There is, however, a difference between telling one-off lies on occasion and being a pathological liar. To start with, pathological liars lie more frequently, telling an average of 10 lies daily (Curtis & Hart, 2020).

Further, pathological lying usually has some common traits. They are as follows.

Elements of Truth

Most pathological liars don't tell outright lies. They add elements of truth to their lies to make them more credible and believable. For instance, they may have a common cold, but they will tell their co-workers that they have COVID symptoms or lay claim to another serious health condition.

Pyramid of Lies Without Pressure

Pathological liars build one lie on top of another without any immediate pressure. A person who repeatedly lies about an extramarital affair cannot be called a pathological liar. They built a pyramid of lies because they wanted to keep their affair a secret. On the other hand, pathological liars lie even when nothing is at stake.

Internal Motivation

For pathological liars, the motive for their falsehood is usually internal, and not external. Lying about work experience, for instance, has external motivation. The external motivation in that case is the person's desire to boost their profile. Self-protection, avoiding danger or embarrassment, etc., are also examples of external motivations for lying.

Conversely, the motive for pathological lying is often internal. Attention seeking, self-esteem issues, wanting to play smart, and so on, are examples of the internal motivations behind pathological lying.

Insight

Insight refers to having a sense of judgment. A person who has insight recognizes that they are doing something wrong or abnormal. Pathological liars usually have insight. They are aware that what they are saying is untrue.

Anyone with a mental health condition that prevents them from knowing that they are lying cannot qualify as a pathological liar. These include people who have bipolar disorder, grandiose delusions, false memory syndrome, and other similar conditions.

Indiscriminate Lying

Pathological liars do not target specific people. They lie to anyone and about anything, including minor events. They are often not bothered about being caught, so they may lie even when the truth is obvious. Pathological liars are, however, still very subtle, like wolves in sheep's clothing.

In the chapters that follow, we look at five ways to improve your narcissistic tendencies through:

- *Mindfulness*—mindfulness is a technique that will teach you how to be present and to accept the moment for what it is, which will allow inferior complexes and expectations of others to subside as well as working with your narcissistic urges.

- *Focusing on gratitude*—this will teach you to be grateful and to reciprocate the energy of another person.

- *Going outwards instead of inwards*—chapter four encourages you to practice self-compassion instead of self-promotion.

- *Cognitive behavioral therapy*—this is a technique widely used by therapists to transform thoughts and behaviors that negatively impact the self.

- *Reparenting the inner child*—this strategy helps you uncover traumas and gives you an opportunity to reparent yourself so that the inner child is happy and allows the adult version of yourself to flourish.

2

Wolf in Sheep's Clothing

Many people think that lies are always straightforward, but they are not. Liars do not always tell outright lies. Since the goal of lying is to get people to accept the lie as truth, liars must present a lie in a way that makes it convincing and acceptable. Invariably, the skillfulness of a liar is in how well they can blur the line between truth and lie.

Pathological liars are wolves in sheep's clothing. They have mastered the art of lying and are very good at it. You can hardly tell when they are saying the truth from when they are lying. That reality is what bothers the victims of pathological liars the most.

I remember when Stacy walked into my office a few years ago. She knew that her son lied so much and wondered why he was so dishonest. Her biggest issue, however, was that she could not tell when he was lying from when was being honest. She wanted me to coach her in that area.

Stacy's son, Raymond, had called her several times to ask for financial help, claiming to have an emergency. She later discovered that he lied to her on many of those occasions. Another time, he asked her for money to treat a sickness, and she declined. He was later admitted to the hospital and placed on life support for weeks.

The doctors said the case would not have deteriorated if Raymond had treated the disease earlier, so Stacy felt responsible for her son's predicament. She felt horrible and almost hated herself for ignoring her son when he needed her help. However, on the flip side, she knew that he still could not be trusted. Hence, she wished there was a mechanism to discern when he was lying to her.

Are You Lying to Me?

There has been extensive research on how to spot a lie. However, experts maintain that the two most vital factors in spotting a lie are lapses from the liar and the instincts of the receiver. The former is the number one factor because the best way to catch a liar is through the loopholes in their story and body language giveaways. Conversely, the latter is the instinctive ability of the receiver to recognize that some parts of the story do not add up and seem suspicious.

Liars are so subtle that only about 55% of lies are discernible (Edwards, 2013). That means 45% of lies have no significant loopholes for anyone to accurately spot them. Moreover, of the 55% of lies that one can accurately discern, another 37% go undetected because of lapses in the receiver's instincts. That means only 18% of lies are detected.

What then are your chances of spotting a lie? Professional investigators and psychology experts have provided tips and guidelines for identifying when someone is lying to you.

Nonverbal Cues for Detecting Lies

Noncongruent Body Gestures

Liars sometimes say something with their mouths while their body movement is saying another thing. For instance, they may say "No" while slightly nodding their head as if to say "Yes." They may point to the right while telling someone to turn left. Such noncongruent body gestures may indicate a lie.

Speech Pattern Changes

An irregular speech pattern is a major telltale sign that someone is lying. Criminal profilers and investigators use this while questioning suspects. They note the times when the suspect's speaking pattern and mannerisms change. Such changes may indicate a lie.

To use this tip, you must first identify the person's regular speech pattern and mannerisms. Do that by asking them familiar, straightforward questions. You can move from there to ask them more challenging questions and watch out for any speech pattern changes.

Examples of speech pattern changes include talking faster, raising their voice, and so on. Usually, the liar returns to their regular speech pattern immediately after the lie.

Unusual Vocal Tone Changes

Unusual vocal tone changes may also expose a liar, subject to their cultural context. For instance, research shows that Chinese people speak with an elevated pitch when they lie. Conversely, Hispanics lower their vocal pitch while lying (Matsumoto & Hwang, 2020).

Eye Direction

Eye contact is one of the indices of truthfulness. Liars often avoid eye contact. Instinctively, it feels like you can see through their eyes and spot the lies, so they avoid eye contact in an attempt to hide the truth.

It is important to note that habitual liars try to maintain eye contact. They know that people know this tip, so they are conscious of it. However, if you watch closely, there will still be slipups once in a while.

Excessive Fidgeting

Kids often fidget a lot while telling lies. You may notice their hands shaking or see them looking at their fingernails and licking their lips while lying. These signs may be less obvious in adults, but you can still pick grooming behaviors and other signs of excessive fidgeting when they lie.

Adults sometimes play with their noses, hairs, or ears while lying. They may also press their fingers to their lips while playing with it. These are unconscious attempts to calm their anxiety and nervousness while lying. Watch out for them, as well as other subtle signs when you suspect that someone may be lying to you.

False Reflections

Many people place their hands on their mouths, eyes, or forehead while reflecting. Others close their eyes to reflect on a question before answering. These are normal gestures when the question requires serious thinking and reflection before answering. Anyone that exhibits these signs before answering a question that does not require deep thinking may be lying.

Shifting Eyes

Shifting or wandering eyes have been associated with lying for a long time, but psychologists now say it is not an absolute telltale sign. Shifting eyes show that a person is trying to remember something. Shifting eyes is normal if the question warrants a long-term memory recall. However, if the question requires no such thing, shifting eyes may indicate lying.

The Place of Cultural Bias in Nonverbal Cues

Cultural bias is very important when you are assessing nonverbal cues for lying. For instance, Indians shake their heads in affirmation and nod in denial. So, an Indian is likely to nod their head while saying "No," and that would be correct in their cultural context. An American that does the same may be lying.

Some cultures also consider direct eye contact to be dubious. In such cultures, it depicts a measure of boldness that chronic liars often exude. Consider these cultural biases when applying the above tips.

Verbal Cues for Detecting Lies

Vague Stories or Information

Liars are often careful of giving too many details. They shy away from revealing details and only give vague answers when asked questions. Their initial story may seem detailed, but they begin to gradually back out when you ask them to tell you more.

Criminal investigators watch out for this sign when reviewing phone call transcripts and witness statements. Do you remember how Stacy doubted her son Raymond's story? She could have used this tip to detect if he was lying or telling the truth. Asking for more details about his health condition and what the doctor said about it could have revealed the truth. Since Raymond was not a doctor, he would have had little to no details to offer if he was lying.

Giving Too Many Details

Liars do this when there is an element of truth in what they are saying. It is common for pathological liars to whip so many unnecessary details around a simple truth when trying to exaggerate or twist the truth to suit their purpose.

When you suspect that someone is lying to you, follow your instincts. Identify the main point in what they are saying and evaluate how many unnecessary details they used to embellish that main point.

If Raymond is sick and needs money to treat the sickness, that's the main point. He would stick to that and tell Stacy how important it is to get prompt treatment. Conversely, a liar would embellish that story with how much pain and discomfort they feel, giving several unnecessary details. They may go on to tell you how wicked and inconsiderate you would be if you refuse to help them.

How to Spot a Liar

Beyond just spotting individual lies, how do you spot a liar? How do you know who to trust and who to watch? Here are a few indicators.

• Someone who claims to be a good liar is likely a liar indeed. That self-identification is enough reason to suspect them.

• Suspect people who repeat almost all questions before answering. Liars often need more time to process their answers, so they buy time by repeating questions.

• Watch out for people who answer questions with half sentences or sentence fragments. Liars often give brief or summarized answers where details are necessary.

Use Your Discretion

These signs are effective for catching liars and detecting lies, but you cannot use them in isolation. The cultural context and the exact circumstance determine whether or not you should use these signs as evidence of lying. Moreover, watch out for multiple signs and follow your instincts.

Further, before you conclude that someone is lying to you, add some pressure by asking them questions that will tax them mentally and make lying more challenging. You may ask them to repeat what they told you in reverse order. Watch out for inconsistencies and other signs of lying that you didn't notice earlier.

Depending on the situation, you may wish to confront the person with the truth or inform them that you doubt what they are saying. Again, watch out for how they respond and see if it matches how liars react when you expose them. You may refer to chapter one for that.

On The Sly

Some liars are so good that you can hardly catch them. They sometimes lie on the sly, so you can't pin anything on them. How do you approach such situations where someone just evades your questions, tells you a half-truth, embellishes the truth, or twists it for their selfish interests? Are these the same as lying? Are they signs of a pathological liar? If not, where do we draw the line?

Avoided Truth vs. Lying

Jason and Helen recently walked into my office to seek help for their relationship crisis. When they met two years ago, Helen pretended to love action movies because Jason loved them. Jason just realized she didn't love action movies and started doubting everything he believed about her. He thinks she is a pathological liar.

Helen didn't lie to Jason, but she had deceived him. She never told him that she loved action movies, but she played along to keep the relationship lively. What she did doesn't make her a pathological liar. However, the deception and how long it lasted are affecting her relationship. Jason is pained that he thought he was about to marry a person she was not.

A person may hide something from you to avoid negative reactions or consequences. While that is a form of deception, it is not the same as lying. Liars distort the truth, while deceivers sometimes just hide the truth. Both, however, have the same intention and may have similar detrimental effects on relationships.

Omitted Truth vs. Lying

Omitted truth is another form of passive deception. Imagine you want to marry someone who cannot have kids, but they never mentioned it to you. They kept quiet about their condition even when you talked about your dream family and how many kids you wish to have. How would you feel?

Leaving out such a vital piece of information provided a false perspective. The failure to correct the pre-existing misconceptions in your mind further worsens the situation. Based on these premises, some experts argue that omitted truth is a form of lying. Some others insist that it's not a form of lying, but they agree that whoever omits the truth is not being transparent.

Most people who omit the truth do so out of fear, guilt, or shame. There is usually an external motivation for the omission. That is not typical of pathological liars. Pathological liars may also omit the truth from time to time, but they often do so to manipulate people's responses and gain sympathy, respect, or attention.

Exaggerated Truth vs. Lying

"This is the best meal ever" is a form of exaggerated truth, but it is harmless. We all use exaggerations like that in day-to-day conversations. The aim is usually to make a story juicier or decorate information with fanciful details to make it more attractive.

However, liars can use exaggerations to deceive people in order to serve their selfish interests. The lies they tell are not the same as mere embellishments. Pathological liars, for instance, use exaggerations out of habit. They embellish stories to portray themselves as heroes or make themselves look like poor victims.

Their intent is usually not to make the story more attractive or interesting. They use exaggerations to deceive, influence, or persuade people. Moreover, pathological liars do not just exaggerate existing stories, but they also craft and exaggerate stories that never happened.

Twisted Truth vs. Lying

Liars use twisted truth a lot when they lie on the sly. They subtly use creative words to twist the narrative for their selfish interests. They manipulate people by creating an illusion of truth with their twisted version. Pathological liars and skilled manipulators often lie in this manner.

Derek and Priscilla were on the verge of breaking up when they came to see me. The issue was about Priscilla's son, Andre. Derek said Priscilla never told her she had a son, whereas Priscilla claimed she told him from the beginning.

This was the story: After a few dates, Derek noticed that Andre was a part of Priscilla's life and asked her if he was her son. Priscilla answered, "It wouldn't be wrong to call him my son. He has been that and more to me."

Priscilla didn't lie, did she? She told the truth but didn't tell the truth. Pathological liars do that habitually and for no obvious reason. They would twist the truth even when there is nothing at stake.

With a pathological liar, the truth is not the truth, and a lie is usually not a straightforward, outright lie. It is more complicated than that, and the line gets somewhat blurry at times. It leaves us to wonder, what is the motive? Why do they lie compulsively even when they stand to lose nothing? That is what the next chapter of this book addresses.

3

What's the Motive?

32

Regardless of the motives behind it, lying is a skill every human seems to naturally possess. Nobody can lay claim to being 100% honest since they were born. We all have an inborn capacity for falsehood and dishonesty.

The propensity for deception is deeply woven into the fabric of our humanity, and we cannot deny that fact. As such, the number one motive for lying is to satisfy the innate desire to work for our self-interests. However, we cannot use that as a justification for lying.

A client once told me about their struggle with a spouse that lies habitually. The lying spouse always justifies his actions with these words: "Baby, I was born this way." The client asked me if their spouse's excuse was valid. Are pathological liars born that way or is lying a learned behavior that they developed somewhere along the line?

Baby, I Was Born This Way

While the initial motivating factor for telling lies in childhood years originates from nature, habitual lying draws its motivation from nurture. Don't ever think that you have problems with pathological lying because you were born that way. Let us explore some of the research studies on this matter.

Bella DePaulo: We Are Natural-Born Liars

Psychologists have long recognized that lying is ubiquitous. Over 20 years ago, the psychologist, Bella DePaulo, conducted a research study with her colleagues using 147 adults as their sample population. They asked each of them to note all the times they lied in one week. The research showed that these people told an average of one to two lies daily (Bhattacharjee, 2017).

Most of the lies were, however, harmless. They included excuses for not doing what they ought to have done, attempts to hide inadequacies, and protecting other people's feelings. For instance, one of the participants failed to dispose of the garbage. In their defense, they claimed that they didn't know where the garbage should go.

There were, however, serious lies too. Someone claimed that his father was a diplomat. He presented a false image to boost his social status. On the extreme, one person admitted to falsifying documents, and another was hiding an extramarital affair.

The research showed that the natural inclination of humans is to protect our interests even when we have to lie to do so. It demonstrated that lying is first a human trait.

Kang Lee: Lying Gets Worse With Age

Kang Lee wanted to know if age affects the rate of lying, so he and his team researched children and how they lie. They hid toys and asked the children to guess which toy was there. They then left the children in the room unsupervised for a few minutes and asked them not to peek.

Lee and the team watched with a monitoring camera and discovered that most of the children could not resist peeking. Further, many of them lied about peeking, but older children told more lies. Here are the figures:

- 30% of the two-year-olds lied about peeking.
- About half of the three-year-olds peeked and lied about it.
- 80% of the eight-year-olds who peeked claimed that they did not (Bhattacharjee, 2017).

What's more, older kids were smarter and more cunning with their lies. Kids between the ages of three and four just blurted out the answer. They didn't realize that the way they answered could reveal their transgression and lie. Conversely, kids between ages seven and eight tried masking their lies by not giving the correct answer.

Kids between ages five and six fell somewhere in the middle of the spectrum. One of them peeked and denied doing so. When it was time to guess, the kid asked if she could touch the toy. After touching it, she gave the correct answer. She did not only hide the lie, but she also made efforts to sound convincing.

Lee's research shows that lying is a learned behavior that people master over time. While lying is an inborn ability, nobody is born a smart liar. That also means nobody is born a pathological liar.

Dan Ariely: We Have Lying Limits

Dan Ariely is a leading psychologist with one of the most extensive research works on lying worldwide. He admits that lying is ubiquitous but wonders why people don't lie more than they do. He thinks that since lying is a natural trait, what stops us from going all the way? Why does the average person still make efforts to be honest?

In one of his research studies, his team gave people the chance to make money from cheating. He realized that the volunteers could not bring themselves to cheat beyond a certain level. They decided to significantly raise the amount of money, but the volunteers still did not go beyond their limits (Bhattacharjee, 2017).

Ariely's research shows that we have an in-built restraint against lying. That internal restraint stops the average person from lying with reckless abandon. A possible factor for that restraint is the value that society places on honesty. Our subscription to some sort of moral code also plays a significant role.

Ariely concluded from his research that the average human places a limit on how far they can go with lying. Only sociopaths have no such limits. As such, the inborn propensity to lie does not justify pathological liars who typically do not have limits. The outcome of Ariely's research suggests that such people may be sociopaths suffering from mental health conditions.

Mental Health and Pathological Lying

Some mental illnesses can indeed make people more prone to lying. Personality disorders top the list of such mental conditions. Experts say that people with personality disorders (narcissistic, antisocial, etc.) might attempt to manipulate and deceive others without regard for the consequences of their actions. Therefore, pathological lying may signify an underlying mental disorder.

Some psychiatrists disagree with the proposition that mental health has links with lying. However, mainstream psychiatrists have observed how people with certain mental health disorders have similar lying behaviors. For instance, narcissists usually lie to increase their self-worth and public image while people with antisocial disorders manipulate with their lies.

Yaling Yang: Evidence From Brain Scan

In 2005, Yaling Yang led a group of psychologists to compare the brain of habitual liars with others. They used brain scans to observe the link between lying and the condition of the brain. The participants were all adults.

- Twelve of the participants were habitual liars.
- Thirty-seven of them were not habitual liars. Sixteen out of these thirty-seven had antisocial disorders, while the remaining twenty-one were not antisocial.

To start with, the sample selection shows that some people have an antisocial disorder but are not habitual liars. That means personality disorders are not a sentence to habitual lying.

Now, to the results. The brain scans showed that habitual liars had 20% or more volume of neural fibers in the prefrontal cortex than others (Bhattacharjee, 2017). That means they had more connections between their brain cells. Some experts say that the richer connections explain why habitual liars could readily cook up lies. Others, however, say that the richer connections were a result of habitual lying.

Nobuhito Abe and Joshua Greene: Lying Causes Brain Changes

The renowned psychologists, Abe and Greene, agree with the notion that habitual lying causes brain changes. They scanned for brain activity in habitual liars and non-habitual liars to evaluate that notion. The scan showed that the nucleus accumbens of habitual liars had more neural activities (Bhattacharjee, 2017). The nucleus accumbens is a part of the brain that plays a vital role in processing rewards.

That result suggests that most habitual liars get a sense of reward and satisfaction from lying. The thing(s) that excite their reward system motivates them to lie. For instance, you are more likely to lie for monetary gain if money excites your reward system.

This research supports the idea that the internal kick pathological liars get from lying is the source of their motivation. Further, it shows that lying can become addictive. One lie leads to another lie, and then several other lies because the reward center gets excited with each lie and seeks that excitement more frequently.

Pathological lying may develop from that vicious cycle. Consequently, the pathological liar feels less and less remorse for lying and lies more smoothly without any internal inhibition.

Tali Sharot: Lying Repeatedly Numbs Our Emotions

Sharot and his team of neuroscientists evaluated the effect of lying on the brain. They watched out for neural activity in the amygdala as the participants lied. The amygdala is the part of the brain that processes emotions.

The research showed that neural activities in the amygdala became weaker with each lie (Bhattacharjee, 2017). That means the brain of habitual liars adjusts and insulates itself against the emotional discomfort and stress that accompany lying. As such, each lie makes it easier to tell more lies. These results lend themselves to the opinion that pathological lying is a learned behavior.

Furthermore, bigger lies did not cause more activity in the amygdala of those who had lied repeatedly, including those who told only small lies. That means small lies now and then often lead to bigger lies without remorse.

The findings from Sharot's research make it seem like we should avoid lying altogether, but is that possible? Can we be 100% honest? Are there times when we should make exceptions and lie notwithstanding its effect on the brain? Are some situations worth the lie?

Worth the Lie?

There are indeed high stakes each time you lie, and that's enough to make anyone want to embrace radical honesty. However, sometimes, there are higher stakes. Lies are sometimes necessary to safeguard your well-being. You can make exceptions and justify lying in such situations. They include:

• Protecting yourself or someone else from abuse by lying to the abuser.

• Escaping death or danger by lying to find a way out.

• Safeguarding children from child abuse by lying to their abuser.

• Lying to a child who is fiddling with a dangerous weapon to get it out of their hands.

• Lying to people who are drunk or intoxicated with drugs.

• Lying to people who have mental health problems to protect their dignity.

Truth is especially delicate for people with severe cognitive decline. Experts say that being blunt with people suffering from severe dementia can cause fear and agitation, and make their condition worse. Psychologists recommend careful and mindful lies that don't undermine trust when dealing with such people.

Honesty is a virtue that we must uphold at all times, but we must recognize special situations that call for an exception. Strive for honesty in all you do, but use your discretion and recognize when lying is the right thing to do.

A Delicate Balance

The idea that some situations are worth the lie presents a peculiar challenge. How do you recognize such situations? Where do you draw the line? How do you strike the balance?

People generally believe that white lies are acceptable because they don't hurt anyone. That means most people judge the morality of a lie based on its motive.

I remember when a friend relocated to another state when he left home. Things were rough for him in the first few weeks there, but he didn't tell anybody at home.

His parents called to find out how he was doing, and he told them he was having a great time. He didn't want them to be worried or bothered about him. Thankfully, everything was okay by the end of his first month there, and he was happy that he didn't give his parents sleepless nights.

In that situation, my friend lied because he cared about his parents. He thought about their feelings and lied out of kindness and empathy. That was a well-intentioned, prosocial lie.

Antisocial lies deplete trust levels and negatively affect relationships. Conversely, prosocial lies build trust and strengthen relationships. The difference between antisocial and prosocial lies is where you draw the line.

What Are Antisocial Lies?

Antisocial lies usually have selfish motives. They are very damaging because they promote your interests without regard for how it affects others. In other words, what you say does not make a lie antisocial. The motive behind the lie determines whether it is an antisocial or prosocial lie.

Imagine that you are attending a party with your best friend. She turned to you after dressing up and asked if the dress looked good on her. You felt the dress was tight because she gained some weight, but you told her it looked great on her.

That could be a prosocial or antisocial lie, depending on the motive. Lying to your friend because you don't want to bruise her ego, self-esteem, or confidence is prosocial. Conversely, lying because you are in competition with her and wish to outshine her at the party is antisocial.

Evaluate Your Lies

Sometimes, the line between antisocial and prosocial lies gets blurry. I usually recommend a two-step evaluation process to help my clients gain clarity. Here are the two factors to consider in differentiating an antisocial lie from a prosocial lie.

Who Will Benefit From the Lie?

Someone who is lying to their spouse about their extramarital affair benefits from the lie. They don't have to own up to their transgression and can continue the affair as long as it remains a secret. That is an example of an antisocial lie.

On the other hand, prosocial lies benefit the listener rather than the liar. Imagine that a close friend has a terminal disease and is about to die. Telling your three-year-old about your friend's impending death will do the child no good. Moreover, such conversations are not appropriate for the child's age.

You can, therefore, protect your child from emotional trauma by lying to them about the impending death. Such a lie is prosocial because it is for the child's benefit. It reflects compassion, empathy, and kindness.

What Will Happen if the Truth Comes Out?

Think of someone who is lying to their spouse about an affair. What will happen if the truth comes out? They will feel embarrassed, and the truth will negatively affect their relationship. The spouse will feel hurt, their marriage might become strained, the children might hate them for cheating, and so on. The consequences are indeed far-reaching.

Most antisocial lies have far-reaching consequences if the truth ever comes out. On the other hand, prosocial lies have little to no consequence if the truth comes out. So, ask yourself, will people detest you when they find out the truth? Do you risk facing any punishment if the truth comes out? Are there long-term negative effects on your life, relationships, career, etc.?

Think about the person who lies to their child about their friend's imminent death. What is at stake if and when the child later finds out the truth? There are no dire consequences. Such is the case with prosocial lies.

"Who will benefit from the lie?" is a question of morality. On the other hand, "What will happen if the truth comes out?" is a question of social acceptance. In summary, after considering the morality of a lie, also consider its social acceptance.

Conclusions on Pathological Lying

Pathological lying is largely a product of nurture and not nature. Moreover, it has antisocial traits and lacks the internal inhibition that average liars have. Therefore, no excuse can justify pathological lying. It is morally wrong and socially unacceptable.

Further, pathological liars lie so often that their brain has adapted to the behavior. The reward center in their brain can become addicted to the security and comfort that lying gives them.

As such, they will lie even when there is no good reason to be dishonest. At that level of dishonesty, their well-being, valuable relationships, and the feelings of others become inconsequential. Pathological liars become emotionally numb to the adverse effects of their behavior.

It is necessary to mention here that the antisocial tendencies of pathological liars are not mutually exclusive to love. A pathological liar can genuinely love people, but that is not enough to keep them in check. They would still find it hard to maintain honesty in the relationship. That is why pathological liars often have toxic relationships filled with emotional stress and hurt for their partners.

If you struggle with pathological or compulsive lying habits, you should seek professional help. If you think a mental illness contributes to the condition, speak with your primary provider, get a diagnosis, and start treatment, if necessary.

Those struggling with compulsive lying must realize the adverse effects of their habit, admit that there is a problem, accept that they need help, and get help where it is available. In other words, they need to face the music.

4

Time to Face the Music

Lying can create serious problems. To start with, lying causes cognitive depletion in liars and increases the risks of negative consequences when the lies are exposed. Cognitive decline means that the brain is becoming less functional and effective. Moreover, since most habitual liars don't see themselves as good people, lying is injurious to self-worth (Preuter et. al, 2021). Instead, it breeds guilt and contempt.

Lying erodes trust in society at large and destroys social networks. If you lie compulsively, you must come to terms with the reality of how much damage your lies can cause. That is vital because it can strengthen your motivation to turn a new leaf.

Lies Break Relationships

Lies and secrets break trust and damage relationships, sometimes beyond repair. This is not just about black or antisocial lies. Even white lies are inimical to the survival and growth of intimate relationships.

It is okay to say, "I'm fine" when a random person asks, "How are you?" You should, however, not do that in an intimate relationship if you want that relationship to last. Be honest about how you feel and what is going on with you. Vulnerability helps build and strengthen intimacy.

Further, you can gush over a gift you dislike if it is from an acquaintance, but you should not do that in an intimate relationship. Such relationships require emotional honesty. If you pretend about what you love and dislike, your partner will not know you for who you are.

Lies of all kinds lead to broken relationships in the long run. Therefore, you should not withhold necessary information and your true feelings from those with whom you share an intimate relationship. They have a right to know, and robbing them of that right can affect your relationship.

Prosocial Lies Also Have Negative Consequences

Prosocial lies are justifiable, but they also have downsides. For example, telling a lie because you don't want to hurt somebody's feelings can help improve your relationship with that person and project you as a trustworthy person. You may, however, be robbing them of objective opinions that can help them make better choices in life.

For instance, why should you lie to your friend whose dress is tight and tell her that her dress is perfect? You may do that out of compassion and to prevent her from feeling bad about adding weight. However, withholding the truth from her may give her false confidence about her weight. Rather than take steps to achieve her desired weight, you will make her live in the illusion that she is already there.

Does that mean you should tell the harsh truth? No, it doesn't. However, it means you can find better ways to present the truth. You can tell your friend that the dress looks good, but it will look better if she sheds a few pounds.

The point is that you must think deeply before telling any lie, including prosocial lies. Prosocial lies are justifiable, but they also have negative effects on the person being lied to. Moreover, remember that prosocial lies cause similar brain changes in liars as antisocial lies.

How Compulsive Lying Affects Relationships

Frankly speaking, most people lie because being honest and vulnerable has its attendant risks, but dishonesty is far riskier. Moreover, if white and prosocial lies negatively affect relationships, you can imagine the damaging effects of pathological lying.

Here are some of the ways pathological lying may affect your relationships.

Pathological Lying Hinders Real Intimacy

Authenticity and trust are the foundations for real intimacy. Do you remember the story of Jason and Helen? Helen pretended that she loved action movies for two years. Jason felt they were bonding over that shared interest, but it was all an illusion. Helen was not authentic, and that prevented her from building real intimacy with Jason.

Can you imagine a relationship with several such lies? A pathological liar has told several lies, building one on top of the other over time. Any kind of intimacy they seem to be building on those lies is nothing but an illusion. It is fake intimacy and cannot stand the test of time.

Pathological Lying Creates Hurdles in Relationships

Each compulsive lie you tell creates a hurdle in the future of your relationship. These hurdles mount up as you tell more lies to cover up the previous one(s). They, however, often seem nonexistent until the truth comes out.

Each time your lies are exposed, you face a hurdle in your relationship. The feeling of betrayal and breach of trust on the part of the deceived partner puts them in a difficult situation. The innocent partner may question everything they've ever believed.

Grievous secrets, long-term deceptions, and repeated exposures create the greatest hurdles. Sadly, some relationships end because the hurdles are either too high or have become too many.

Pathological Lying Creates Distance

Compulsive liars may feel uncomfortable about topics and discussions that can expose their lies and secrets. Those who have several secrets may even feel uncomfortable about closeness and any form of intimate conversation. These reactions are often unconscious.

Dave and Clara came to see me a few months ago. These two lovebirds were having a hard time in their relationship. During one of the sessions, Dave admitted that the problem was with him. He said he had been avoiding Clara for no reason. He didn't want to spend as much time with her as they used to.

Clara felt Dave was no longer in love with her, but Dave claimed that he still loved Clara very much. Why then was he so preoccupied with his friends, hobbies, and work? Why was he making out little to no time for private moments with Clara? It turned out to be the subconscious effects of his compulsive lies.

Lies Damage Family Relationships

Lying has the following negative effects on family relationships.

Self-Doubt

Compulsive liars create confusion for other members of the family. The lies can make them question their sanity sometimes. The pathological liar paints a different picture from the real story and makes others wonder if they truly see, feel, or hear things correctly. Family members that face these kinds of lies constantly can develop self-doubt problems.

Harmful Legacies

Children can quickly pick up their parent or caregiver's harmful behaviors. As such, if one parent lies compulsively, the children are likely to develop the same habit. Experts call this phenomenon modeling.

Modeling is the phenomenon whereby unhealthy interactions and behaviors within the family system imprint on the children. Modeling is responsible for how children often mimic or repeat the bad habits and behaviors of their parents in adulthood. That means refusal to get help for pathological lying can endanger the future of generations yet unborn. Lying would then become a hurtful family pattern that passes from generation to generation through modeling. Other negative effects of lies on the family include:

- distrust of the compulsive liar
- lack of a strong family bond
- resentment towards the compulsive liar
- fabricated or distorted family history by the compulsive liar

Lies Negatively Affect Friendships

Friends feel betrayed when you lie to them and they find out. While your family may stick with you and tolerate your bad behavior, friends may not do that. They are likely to walk away since they can no longer trust you.

Lying is not good, but doing it repeatedly is extremely hurtful. Friends feel left out, kept in the dark, and alone when they realize that many things they thought they knew about their friends were lies. Just a couple of lies exposed will make them question all the happy moments in the friendship. Joyful memories would quickly fade into the dark clouds and may turn into anger and rage.

Lies Destroy Romantic Relationships

Lying to a romantic partner is dangerous. To start with, everyone wants a partner that gets them. We all want a partner that truly knows us and understands us. How will you get such a partner if you lie to them every time? A romantic relationship built on constant lies is dead on arrival. It is bound to crash in the long run.

Furthermore, liars find it hard to trust others. A compulsive liar would often project their deceptive tendencies onto their partner. They often suspect that their partner is not being completely honest. That attitude can quickly become toxic and damage the relationship.

Lies Compromise Work-Related Relationships

Every establishment has business ethics and guidelines. When you lie at work, management would evaluate the severity of your lie and its impact. That would, in turn, determine the appropriate disciplinary action for your behavior. Some lies can cost you your job.

Lies can also affect collaboration and teamwork. Your colleagues may have a hard time working with you if you have a reputation for lying. That can affect the productivity of your team.

Moreover, your colleagues can deploy the law to deal with you. I remember the story of a man who faced a lawsuit for defamation of character. He made a mistake and lied that his colleague made the mistake. He thought everything would end there, but management decided to serve the colleague a query letter. After replying to the query letter, that colleague sued him for defamation of character and won the suit.

Lies Have Negative Effects on the Recipients

Lies have negative emotional and psychological effects on people who are constantly lied to. Here are some of those effects.

They Develop Trust Issues

The most apparent effect of lying is that it erodes trust. When a person's trust keeps suffering blows upon blows, they start finding it difficult to trust again. They not only stop trusting the person that lied to them repeatedly, but they also find it difficult to trust other people.

They Feel Disrespected

Truth, no matter how insignificant it seems, is a sign of respect. People feel respected when they know that you will never lie to them, no matter the situation. It shows that you value your relationship with them and you don't want to risk jeopardizing it with a lie.

Lies show the opposite. If you lie to someone constantly, they feel highly disrespected. Your constant lies would make them feel like you do not value your relationship with them and don't care if it is jeopardized.

Conversations Become Stressful

Once a person finds out you lied to them, they would expect you to lie again. They would become unsure of what to believe and what not to believe when you are talking. Your lies may make them start questioning every statement you make. They would literally scrutinize your words for any trace of dishonesty. These make conversations more stressful and mentally taxing.

Staying in the relationship would mean a constant rush of stress hormones through their blood. That could make them age faster and cause a host of other health problems.

They May Feel Like a Fool

Realizing that you have been constantly lied to and deceived is not pleasant at all. People often wonder if they are that foolish or gullible when they find out that they believed so many lies for so long. They may feel stupid for falling for those lies. These are painful feelings that one cannot forget in a hurry.

They Feel Cheated

A great relationship requires commitment from both parties. Constant lies can show a lack of commitment and hurt the party that gave their commitment to the relationship. They feel cheated because they put their whole heart into the relationship while the other person held theirs back and lied repeatedly.

They May Feel Justified in Lying

When you repeatedly lie to a person, they may retaliate by lying to you also. Moreover, they would feel less guilty because they are paying you back in your coin. In the end, the entire relationship would become a sham.

Boomerang: Lies Negatively Affect Liars Too

Habitual lying does not only affect the recipients, but it also has unfavorable effects on the liars. Research shows that telling lies has a direct link with increased risks for depression, anxiety, obesity, and cancer (Dooba, 2021).

Telling lies also reduces the risk of overcoming gambling and addiction. Further, lying leads to poor relationships and a lack of work satisfaction. These are in addition to effects like lower self-esteem and emotional numbness that we have seen before.

Addictions

Substance abuse and other forms of addiction are already hard to break. Lying, however, further complicates the situation. People that lie to keep their alcohol or drug use a secret are more likely to use it more. That also reduces their chances of dealing with the problem.

The liar may feel trapped in a loop. They lie because of their addiction. The lies, however, keep them addicted and make the addiction worse. If you are in such a situation, you can break out of the loop by opening up to the right person and seeking the help you need.

Isolation

Liars often become lonely and isolated because nobody wants to keep relating with a liar. If you constantly lie to people, they will distance themselves from you. Meanwhile, the feelings of guilt, shame, and low self-esteem would make you less bold to pursue other relationships.

Shortened Lifespan

Having no genuine friendships or social connections shortens lifespan. It is, therefore, safe to assume that pathological lying can indirectly shorten your lifespan.

Health Problems

Constant lies can affect the health of the liar in several ways. For starters, lying causes anxiety and triggers an increase in blood pressure and heart rate. It leads to a surge of stress hormones, like serotonin, cortisol, and adrenaline, in the blood. These stress hormones have close links with depression, obesity, and some types of cancer (Dooba, 2021).

Remember that compulsive lies tell an average of 10 lies daily. That means an average of 10 stress hormones surge in 24 hours. Such constant exposure to serotonin and other stress hormones decreases longevity and causes a myriad of serious health issues.

Lying Is Stressful

Lying causes a lot of mental stress for the liar. Many liars do not realize this because lying does not require so much physical exertion. However, the brain cares a lot about honesty. We are social animals, and our brains prioritize reputation. That is why most people will do anything to have a good name.

Dishonesty can damage your reputation beyond repair, and your brain knows it. That creates a distressed and perturbed internal state each time you lie. The signals from your brain release stress hormones into your body. These hormones cause some immediate physical reactions like

- faster breathing
- rapid heart rate
- dry mouth

- sweating
- shaky voice

These physical reactions are the bases for polygraph or lie detector tests.

A Frantic Brain

Experts observed from brain imaging tests that the brain is relaxed when a person is being honest, but it is frantic when the person is lying. The brain's limbic system activates the fight or flight reaction similar to what happens during anxiety or a panic attack. One research study even showed that the limbic system becomes so active while telling a lie that it looks like a fireworks display (Sullivan, 2020).

A Lesson From Marta in Knives Out

Have you watched the movie Knives Out? Ana de Armas played the character of Mara in that movie. The character puked each time she lied. Doctors have weighed in on that character, examining whether there could be such a physical reaction to lying.

Many doctors say that they have never seen such a condition. Moreover, there is no such condition as chronic post-lying vomiting. Several doctors have, however, referred to gut-brain communication as a possible cause of that condition.

Gut-brain communication is a two-way interaction between the brain and the digestive system. It is the reason why you get butterflies whenever you are nervous. Dr. Kara Margolis says that the same mechanism can cause nausea and vomiting when there is significant anxiety (Sullivan, 2020).

Marta is, therefore, a picture of the many things that can go wrong when you lie constantly. Suffice it to say that lying causes significant distress and discomfort. Things may, however, not be as dramatic as vomiting after telling a lie.

The Way Forward

Experts once studied the long-term effects of lying on the brain. They realized that liars become more comfortable as they continue lying habitually and wanted to know why. The study showed that the human brain has a great ability to adapt to negative behaviors, including lying and dishonest behaviors.

Tali Sharot experimented on liars and noticed lesser limbic system activities as they continued lying. She concluded that the brain builds tolerance for the shock effects of lying and becomes less bothered by it when a person lies constantly (Sullivan, 2020).

Sharot's research proves once again that each lie you tell makes the next one easier. That explains why small and seemingly insignificant dishonest behavior often escalates into bigger and more significant ones.

Further, since consistent practice can force the brain to adapt to lying, there is less internal motivation to change. That is why society disdains dishonesty. It is the reason why people don't want to give liars another chance when they are caught. It then seems like the only way to motivate people toward honesty is to enforce social rules and penalize liars.

Pathological liars suffer these social penalties all the time with no change in view. What then is the way forward? The pathological liar must sincerely seek a turnaround, otherwise, nothing else will work. In the next chapter, I will share practical strategies that you can use if you are a pathological liar seeking a turnaround.

5

Seeking a Turnaround

If you struggle with pathological lying, and you are sincerely seeking a turnaround, I can recommend a few strategies for you. These strategies have helped several of my clients over the years. There are several strategies, but they all start from the same point: Coming clean.

Coming Clean

Start by coming clean with yourself. Admit to yourself that you have an issue with lying. Until that happens, every effort you make to stop lying pathologically will be futile.

Next, be vulnerable to your partner or the people that you hurt the most with your lies. Open up to them about your struggle. You don't have to tell the whole world that you struggle with pathological lying, but some people need to know.

You need all the support you can get from these people. They include your family, your significant other, and maybe your closest friends. You may seek professional advice if you are not sure about who to tell and who not to tell.

Before we get started on that, however, let's double-check if you really have a lying problem. Let me walk you through how you can come to grips with whether or not you have a problem with lying without being biased about it.

Do You Lie?

Look out for the following signs whenever you are talking to evaluate whether you lie or not. What's more, the frequency with which you do them shows how much you lie.

Contradicting Yourself

Whenever you find yourself telling contradictory stories, it is because you lied in at least one of those stories. If your story is straight, you wouldn't have a hard time keeping the details. You would stick to the same story if they ask you to go over it a thousand times. Even if there are slight variations due to memory lapses, there will be no serious contradictions.

If you lie frequently, you are likely to contradict yourself a lot. If people are always telling you that your stories are contradictory, you likely lie a lot.

Hiding Verifiable Details

Liars often try to hide verifiable details so that nobody can probe further. If you find yourself avoiding verifiable details whenever you talk, it may be because you add falsified information to your stories. Giving no verifiable details prevents anyone from proving or disproving whatever you have said and makes it easy to keep lies undiscovered.

Overly Dramatic Stories

Liars, especially habitual liars, love telling long and dramatic stories. If you have the desire to make your stories longer, more dramatic, and more interesting, you are likely to flesh them out with lies. If you have an anecdote for every intense or dramatic situation, you may have a lying problem.

Average, Prolific, or Compulsive Liar?

The fact that you lie at all does not make you a pathological liar. Lying a lot does not also make you a pathological liar. Some people are prolific liars because they lie a lot, but they do not qualify as pathological liars.

How do average lying and prolific lying compare with pathological lying? Average lying is an expected behavior from the average person. There is hardly a 100% honest person on the earth. On the other hand, pathological lying is a behavioral disturbance. Prolific lying is somewhere in between the two.

- Average liars tell one to two little lies daily and one big lie weekly.
- Prolific liars tell an average of six little and three big lies daily.
- Compulsive liars lie more than ten times daily on average.

Little Lies vs. Big Lies

Examples of little lies include the following:

- Lying because you don't want to hurt another person's feelings. For instance, telling someone "No, you don't suck at dancing." when they feel sad that they embarrassed themselves on the dance floor.

- Lying to defend or protect someone. For instance, telling a creditor that your wife traveled out of town is considered a little lie.

- Lying by saying nice things about a gift you don't like. For instance, "Wow! These dresses look really nice, I love them. Thanks, you made my day."

- Lying to keep a personal secret other than covering up another lie. For instance, telling your friends, "I can't take alcohol because I'm observing lent," whereas you're avoiding alcohol because you're pregnant, but you don't want them to know yet.

- Lying to keep things away from a child. Remember all the boogeyman lies you were told as a child? Those are all under the category of little lies.

Examples of big lies include the following:

- Lying about love. For instance, telling someone that you're in love with them when you're not.

- Lying to your partner about the places you went to or the people you have been with.

- Lying by calling in sick to your workplace when nothing is wrong with you. Some people try to justify this lie by calling it a mental health day off.

- Lying to your significant other about how you are spending money.

- Lying that you were busy when you intentionally ignored a call.

- Lying about how much alcohol you've had.

- Lying by complimenting someone when they don't look good. In this case, nobody asked for your opinion, so you didn't have to say anything.

Prolific Lying Is Nonpathological

Prolific liars are people who lie habitually but still don't meet the criteria for pathological lying. Prolific lying, however, involves lots of deception and results in serious problems too. In my opinion, prolific liars also need to work on their lying habits.

One study by an Oakland university professor observed that prolific liars were mostly young men with high occupational status (Serota & Levine, 2014). Many of them occupy supervisory or managerial positions. That may suggest that prolific liars get ahead easily in life. They, however, have relationship issues with their lovers, families, friends, and coworkers because of their lying habits.

Pathological Liars Tell Outrageous Lies

Pathological liars tell a lot of outrageous lies, and their lies have no clear motives. Unlike prolific liars, there is no evidence that lying helps pathological liars to get ahead in life. Their lies often contain elaborate details that sound too good to be true. What makes the lies even more outrageous is that you can spot many of them with ease. A pathological liar can tell you he's a billionaire, whereas it is clear that he isn't.

Some people argue that pathological lying is a mental disorder. Experts have, however, concluded that it is not. They say it is either just a behavioral disturbance or a manifestation of a personality or brain disorder. Examples of such disorders include antisocial personality disorder, borderline personality disorder, and Korsakoff's syndrome.

So, back to the initial question: Do you have a lying problem? How serious is the lying problem? Do you tell small or big lies? Are you an average, prolific, or pathological liar? Begin your journey to change by coming clean about this to yourself and vital relationships in your life. Thereafter, you can start putting in the effort, and you will see the turnaround that you seek.

Putting in the Effort

Honesty is virtuous and valuable, but it takes effort to become a more honest person. You need even more effort if you already struggle with compulsive lying. However, you must exert effort in the right direction to get the results you desire. In other words, you cannot see the turnaround you seek if you don't focus your efforts on realistic and practical strategies.

Over the years, I have used several tips and strategies to assist my coaching clients in their quest to become more honest. Here are my top strategies that have delivered results.

Be Honest With Yourself

It is easier to lie to others when you successfully deceive yourself or ignore the truth. As such, being honest with yourself is one of the effective ways to break free from the grip of compulsive lying. When you do that, you will find it increasingly easier to be truthful to other people.

Start by examining your feelings and intentions in every situation. How do you feel about the situation? What do you hope to achieve from the conversation? Are your intentions consistent with your feelings? In vital relationships, make sure your intentions in conversations are always consistent with the way you feel.

This strategy worked for Olivia. She knew she had a problem with lying and wasn't sure how to confront it. Olivia told me that she usually would lie before realizing it. That had a lot to do with the fact that she didn't reconcile her feelings with her intentions before starting conversations.

I recommended this strategy to her, and she found it very helpful. In her words, "I realized that it was easier to lie automatically when I wasn't prepared for the conversation." She went on to say, "Evaluating my feelings and intentions before serious conversations brought a measure of intentionality into those conversations."

Understand the Underlying Issues

Most pathological liars are not bad people. You don't lie because you are determined to hurt or betray the people you love. You end up hurting them, but it also hurts you to see them hurt. Why then do you keep lying? Are there certain fears or ideologies that predispose you to lie?

Jake had concerns about his lying habit, so he sought my help. After a few coaching sessions, he realized that he disliked confrontations and arguments. As such, he lied whenever he felt the truth would cause an argument or confrontation.

That soon became a habit and his coping mechanism for difficult situations. He would lie to cover up previous lies and end up with a web of lies. His underlying issue, therefore, was his fear of confrontations and arguments. He focused his effort on overcoming that fear and was able to eventually see the turnaround he was seeking.

In my introduction to this book, I talked about Jack, my client who wished he had a reset button. In his case, he had an underlying assumption that people preferred lies. He felt the need to tell people what they wanted to hear rather than the truth. He realized through our coaching sessions that people preferred to be hurt by the truth than to be betrayed by a lie.

That realization was his reset button. It still took some effort, but he began his journey to change from there and succeeded in the long run.

For some people, their underlying issue is the fear of judgment, the desire to be right, or the need for validation. For some others, it's a health challenge. Once you identify your underlying problem, you know where to start from. Focus your attention on dealing with the underlying problem, and your lying issues will become a thing of the past.

Be Real

You often have to work hard to keep up the image when you have created a persona with your lies. Now that you want to start being honest, you should stop keeping up. That way, you wouldn't have to keep building up lies upon lies anymore. Breaking free from the loop of lies can be the beginning of your turnaround.

I know it is hard to own up to your real self if you have built a false persona over time, but it's worth it. The story of Helen and Jason comes to mind here; I told you about them earlier. Helen had deceived Jason to think that she loves action movies like him. She also built other false personas to keep the relationship going.

In seeking a turnaround, Helen had to come clean to Jason about who she was, the things she liked, and the things she disliked. Being real was the beginning of the process for her. She didn't have to keep pretending or telling more lies anymore.

Come to terms with the fact that not everybody will like you for who you are. Make peace with your flaws and inadequacies; don't go the extra mile to hide them. Just be yourself while you do your best to be a good person.

Practicing Honesty

As in all other things, practice makes perfect when it comes to being honest. Putting efforts to embrace a turnaround does not mean you won't slip up once in a while, but you must continue to practice honesty until it becomes a habit. I recommend six powerful tips for my clients on how to practice honesty. They are as follows.

Admit

No matter how hard you try, it is impossible to change a behavioral disturbance in one day. You may catch yourself lying unintentionally, but don't beat yourself up for it. Admit that you fell off the track and make up your mind to get back on track. Don't hesitate to let your partner know that you lied and tell them the truth about the situation.

What if you're caught lying? I know it's embarrassing, but don't become defensive. Admit that you lied. Face the truth and take in the embarrassment. Accept the consequences of your mistakes. Any attempt to cover up your mistake will send you deeper into the dark hole of lying.

No matter how many times you have to admit to lying, keep doing it. Your loved ones will see that you are making efforts and that you're serious about it. It will help rebuild their trust. They may not yet trust you enough that you will always tell them the truth, but they can confidently say that you will always own up to your mistake.

Apologize

Beyond admitting to your mistake, ensure to apologize. Don't say sorry out of necessity; say sorry because you mean it. Don't shy away from being in a vulnerable position.

Olivia's story is a good case study here. She didn't have a problem admitting to her lies, but she had this habit of blaming her boyfriend, George, for her lies. I coached her to stop doing that, and rather admit that her lies were wrong and unjustifiable. Her relationship became stronger, and she found it easier to improve when she began to practice this tip.

Renew Your Commitment

Vow to yourself never to make the mistake again and let whoever you have hurt know that too. Tell them that you will do your best not to lie to them again. Talk about why you lied in the first place, how you feel about the mistake, and why you know it needs to stop.

Emphasize that you don't wish to keep hurting them with lies. Convince them that you are still committed to change and growth. Renew your commitment to leading an honest life and becoming a better person.

Show Care

Lies can be very hurtful, so show that you care about your partner's feelings when you lie to them. Ask them how they feel and listen to them with rapt attention. Show them that how they feel about your actions is important to you.

Your loved one may have many things to say. Be patient and actively listen for as long as they want to talk. Listening to them talk about their feelings will go a long way in repairing the damage in your relationship. It will solve relational problems while you're on your way to perfection.

During the conversation:

- Ask questions when you need more clarity on what they're saying.
- Encourage them to keep talking and not hold anything back.
- Do not dominate the conversation.
- Allow them to vent if they want to.

Give Them Time

It takes time to rebuild trust when you break it. As such, let your significant other know that you're willing to do what it takes to regain their trust and rebuild the relationship. Give them time and be patient with them as they work through their feelings.

You may feel hurt, frustrated, or ignored in the process, but understand that your significant other is nursing a wound. Respect their feelings and encourage them to keep talking. Let them know how you feel too, but take responsibility. These tips will make your relationship stronger as you come out of the difficult season.

Be Tactful

Honesty without tactfulness is nothing but cruelty. The fact that you are being honest does not mean you can do it anyhow you like. There are tactful ways to say the truth if you don't want it to hurt those you love. Otherwise, you will become frustrated somewhere along the line. It would seem like nothing pays, either saying the truth or telling a lie.

Many of my clients had a challenge in this area. I talked about one of them, Eva, earlier. She was caught in a fix because it felt like her husband hated both lies and truth. She felt like she had to embrace one of two evils, and lying was the easier option. I taught her to be tactful with the truth, and it helped.

How do you apply tact in saying the truth? Think through your words whenever you are saying the truth. Be kind always and speak out of love and care. Seek to be right not only with what you are saying but also with how you are saying it.

Pay attention to this tip especially when the truth is sensitive or risky. I know that honesty may have consequences, no matter how tactful you are. However, be nice still and bear whatever consequences come as a result of the truth.

Take Further Steps

The strategies and tips above are tested and proven, but they may not work in every situation. If you apply them without seeing results, you may need medical intervention. Visit a psychotherapist and ask for professional help. Aside from helping you treat the problem, therapists can also engage with those close to you and help them cope with the challenge better.

In the next chapter, I will talk about the different approaches that experts use in treating pathological lying.

6

Scouting Solutions

68

Personal efforts have helped lots of people overcome their struggles with compulsive lying. However, these efforts are sometimes not enough, and professional help becomes necessary. There is currently no medication for pathological lying, but there are medications to help manage mental health conditions that may cause compulsive lying. Moreover, psychotherapy has proven to be the most effective treatment.

Psychologists and psychotherapists treat people with pathological or compulsive lying, but mainstream experts agree that it is not a psychological disorder. There are arguments here and there, but that is the position of science as of the time of writing this book (Kandola, 2021). As such, there is still no clear-cut treatment regimen for pathological lying.

Observational studies and research show that pathological lying can be a symptom of a mental health disorder. Mental health experts and psychologists treat pathological lying by assessing if there is an underlying mental disorder. Treating the underlying condition usually helps resolve the problem of pathological lying.

No Quick Fix

Some people struggling with compulsive lying think that visiting an expert will give them a quick fix. It is not like a headache that you take medications for and go to sleep. The underlying issue is usually a mental health problem that requires your willingness and cooperation to deal with.

The behavioral specialist or psychotherapist will work with you to diagnose any underlying mental health condition. Further, they will offer therapy and/or medications to help manage the problem. The entire process requires your cooperation and participation.

You may be wondering, what are some of the mental health conditions that cause chronic lying? The potential diagnoses are many, but the common ones are as follows.

Addiction Disorders

There are different sources of addiction, including alcohol, cigarettes, pornography, and gambling. If you are addicted to any of these things or anything else for that matter, you may start lying to keep your addiction a secret. The idea behind telling such lies is so that you wouldn't have to stop the addiction.

Lying about your addiction is a sign that you are ashamed of it. At the very least, it means that you acknowledge that it is socially unacceptable. As such, it is better to come clean and seek professional help for your addiction disorder. You will have no secrets anymore and you won't have to keep up with the lies.

Attention Deficit Hyperactivity Disorder

People with attention deficit hyperactivity disorder (ADHD) often struggle with self-control and impulsivity. They respond more easily to impulses before processing their actions. Therefore, they often lie before they even realize what they did.

I have met several clients who were frustrated with themselves. One of them once told me that he could not explain how his mouth was faster than their brain. That statement was what made me explore the possibility of ADHD. It turned out that was his underlying problem.

Further, people with ADHD find it difficult to consider future consequences in the face of immediate satisfaction or benefits. Such people can also improve through therapy and medical help.

Histrionic Personality Disorder

People who have histrionic disorders often desire attention. They can go to any length, including using lies and dramatic behavior, to gain attention. They get a lot of excitement and satisfaction when they get attention. That internal motivation may explain their unexplainable lying habits. If you notice that you often lie to gain attention, visit a psychotherapist for a proper evaluation to see if you meet the criteria for a histrionic disorder.

Antisocial Personality Disorder

People with antisocial personality disorder constantly disregard people's rights and their personal spaces. They often exploit people, break the law, and exhibit aggressive or reckless behavior. This was the first mental disorder associated with pathological lying. At that time, experts were only researching pathological lying among convicts and suspected criminals.

However, we now know that many people suffer from antisocial disorder without committing crimes. That notwithstanding, they still hurt the people around them by disregarding their right to know the truth. They also disrespect people with their nonchalant attitude toward their emotions.

Antisocial personality disorder is so serious, and many people dread the diagnosis. It has been associated with cruelty and manipulation, but there's more to these behaviors. Personal amusement is the basis for all the antisocial behaviors of people with this disorder. It is also the reason why they lie. They don't behave the way they do because they intentionally seek to hurt people.

If you realize that you lie for personal amusement and with a lot of arrogance, you should be evaluated for antisocial personality disorder. Another red flag for an antisocial disorder is if you notice that you generally care less about people's rights and feelings.

Borderline Personality Disorder

People with borderline personality disorder struggle with mood shifts. They also exhibit an unstable pattern and have self-image issues because of their constant mood shifts. They may lie often to make up for their self-image issues. These issues negatively affect their interpersonal relationships.

Does this describe you? Does it capture why you struggle with compulsive lying? Then you should visit a psychologist for evaluation and therapy.

Factitious Disorder

Experts once called this condition Münchausen syndrome. People with this disorder lie about having a chronic illness to get more attention. They can also lie about psychological or physical symptoms instead of a disease. If you find yourself doing this often, you may be suffering from a factitious disorder.

Anxiety Disorder

Pathological lying is not a definitive symptom of anxiety disorder, just as it is not a hallmark symptom of any mental disorder. However, it is also a common cause of lying problems. People who have anxiety problems may panic and lie when anything triggers their anxiety. They may also lie to avoid rejection or any other things they are anxious about.

You should talk to experts if anxiety is at the root of your lying problems.

Narcissistic Personality Disorder

People who have narcissistic personality disorders (NPD) feel so self-important. They often exaggerate their talents or accomplishments, and that is the origin of their lies. You should consider seeking evaluation for NPD if you show other signs of NPD, such as a lack of empathy, arrogance, and self-centered behavior.

Obsessive Compulsive Disorder

Intrusive feelings, thoughts, and obsessions are common in people with obsessive compulsive disorder (OCD). If you often have a strong urge or compulsion to do certain things or to do things a certain way, you may have OCD. You should see a behavioral specialist for professional help.

OCD can sometimes cause compulsive lying. It can either be the true compulsion of the person suffering from OCD or a coping method for their true compulsion.

Beyond Mental Disorders

I must make it clear here that not all compulsive liars suffer from a mental illness. Some compulsive liars only lie for personal and social reasons. If you are unsure of the reason behind your lies, experts can help you find out. Moreover, psychologists help with other common problems that may cause pathological lying.

Some of the other common problems that behavioral specialists and psychologists can help you with include the following.

Insecurity

People who struggle with insecurity may find themselves lying a lot. They lie to inflate their ego and increase their sense of self-worth or importance. Insecure people also use lies as a defense mechanism against social exclusion or public ridicule.

I remember coaching Pat and Ron in their relationship. Pat came from a rich family but Ron came from a humble background. He often felt insecure when he was around Pat's friends and family, so he started making up stories to prevent exclusion or ridicule. Pat got bothered about his lying habits and suggested that he needed help.

Ron got anxious when any of Pat's friends asked about his childhood, what he was doing for a living and other personal questions. You see, Ron was a good guy with insecurity problems. Once we got past his insecurities, he became a more honest person.

Try to watch the pattern of your lies. Is there a common trend with insecurities? If so, you can seek professional help for the underlying problem.

Reputation

Some people lie because they see no better way to maintain a good reputation. Their lies are, therefore, for social status and nothing else. For instance, Ron's lying problems became worse when Pat encouraged him to join her dad's golf club.

The club was filled with rich men who looked down on people of lesser financial status. They considered their organization prestigious and only super-rich people had a say. As such, Ron had to lie and pretend to fit in and maintain a good reputation in the club.

There were two options in this case. Ron could choose to quit the club or stay, be himself, and care less about people's opinions of him. Ron chose to quit the club, and it helped him become more honest.

Humor

Humor is a less common cause of lying problems than the other two already mentioned above. Some people lie just because they think it's funny. They may think their lies are too obvious for anyone to believe. They may also not understand how much their lies frustrate or hurt the people around them.

The problem with those who lie for humor is that they don't see the problem. As far as they are concerned, they are just catching fun. Professional help may be necessary if you find lying funny and you find it hard to believe that anyone ever took your lies seriously.

Therapy is a good starting point for compulsive liars who can't overcome their lying problems with self-help. Your therapist will help you explore all possible options and dig until you get to the root of the problem. Depending on the diagnosis, the therapist may continue to treat you or refer you to medical experts or mental health specialists for comprehensive treatment.

A Conscious Effort to Change

Therapy does not work like magic. It requires conscious efforts on your part too. Firstly, you must be willing to talk to an expert and open up to them. You will have to tell them the truth about your troubling thoughts, emotions, and behavior.

Moreover, various factors go into the diagnosis and treatment of underlying causes of pathological lying. Several factors also go into assessing the best treatment protocol for each person. You are not likely to push through with the entire process without conscious efforts to change.

The evaluation and treatment processes are not tedious, but they will be a waste of time without the genuine desire and effort toward a more honest living.

I will go over the different treatment options for compulsive lying. Prepare your mind ahead in case your situation requires any of them.

Therapy for Compulsive Lying

Therapy is the most common treatment method for behavioral problems like compulsive lying. Counselors, social workers, psychotherapists, and other mental health professionals use therapy for their clients. The common therapy options for people struggling with pathological lying include the following.

Cognitive Behavioral Therapy

Cognitive behavioral therapy (CBT) focuses on the constant thoughts in your mind, your beliefs and worldviews, and any distortions in thinking. It is the go-to option for many personality disorders. Your therapist may recommend CBT if you are diagnosed with an antisocial, borderline, or narcissistic disorder.

Aversion Therapy

Experts use aversion therapy to recondition the mind. The therapist will guide you to link your unwanted behavior or habit, in this case, compulsive lying, to the unwanted feeling or stimulus. Then, you can learn to suppress that unwanted behavior.

For instance, if you struggle with nail-biting you can link it to a bitter taste. That would help you avoid biting your nails. Using aversion therapy, your therapist may help you link lying to unwanted feelings such as eating worms or wearing rags; whatever works for you.

I have used aversion therapy for several clients, and it works. Once they successfully linked their lying behavior with a feeling they have an aversion to, honesty became easier for them.

Dialectical Behavior Therapy

Therapists can recommend dialectical behavior therapy (DBT) to help regulate emotions in people who struggle with mood shifts or erratic emotions. With DBT, you will be able to better process your emotions and repair broken relationships. It will also help you develop adaptive behaviors in place of compulsive lying.

Schema-Focused Therapy

Schema-focused therapy is used for people who didn't respond to other therapies or those who relapsed after being through CBT or other therapies. It focuses on lifelong behavioral and thinking patterns. Its change techniques are effective, and I have seen it work for several people with compulsive lying problems.

Note that people respond differently to the various therapies above. Moreover, you might try a few times before you find the therapy that works for you. That is where determination comes in.

What the Therapy Process Feels Like

Therapy might initially seem intimidating to those trying it for the first time. You may be a bit nervous about opening up to a stranger. You may also find it awkward that you have to discuss your personal history and struggles with the therapist. It is completely okay to feel that way.

Your therapist owes you the duty to create a comfortable, safe, and enabling environment where you'll feel free to open up and share your experiences. However, a basic understanding of the process may also help calm your nerves.

Basically, therapists aim to gather as much information as possible from you. What they know about you and your situation will help them form a well-informed, holistic opinion about the situation. That would, in turn, help them arrive at an accurate diagnosis.

Questioning

To kick-start the therapy, your mental health provider will ask you various questions. Your answers to these questions will help them understand you better and gain insight into your situation. The questions may include inquiries about the current thoughts, past experiences, and daily feelings that have shaped your worldview.

The therapist may ask why you came for therapy. Take that opportunity to talk about your struggles with lying and its impact on your social and professional relationships. Share your goals and expectations for the treatment.

You cannot give them all the information they need in one day, so there is no pressure whatsoever. You can wait until you are comfortable enough with your therapist to share certain details with them. Your therapists will not coerce you to give them access to the intimate areas of yourself.

Diagnosis

Your therapist might use a few psychological assessment tools during your therapy. These tools typically include a list of questions. Answer them honestly so that your provider will have accurate information to work with. With the proper information they can make a reliable diagnosis and create an effective treatment plan for you.

The psychological assessments might seem like an exam. Note, however, that these are not pass or fail exams. Your honest answers are necessary for the therapist to diagnose the root cause of your lying behavior and the best way to manage it.

Be patient with your therapist. You may have to attend several sessions before they give you a diagnosis. You want an accurate diagnosis rather than a quick fix or trial and error process. Only then will the actual therapeutic process begin.

Management

Professional therapists go beyond offering a diagnosis and leaving you to your fate. Instead, they will hold you by the hand to manage the behavior. They will recommend different coping strategies and behavioral therapy.

Behaviors are not easy to drop. However, you can make consistent progress with solid support from your therapist and loved ones. Honest living, which had been hitherto difficult to attain, will thereafter become easier by the day.

Ensure to find a therapist whose skills match your needs. You need someone you can connect with easily and trust with ease. The therapist should make you feel understood and comfortable. Follow their recommendations, including if they refer you for further medical care.

Medications for Compulsive Lying

Some of the underlying mental health problems causing compulsive lying require medications alongside therapy. For instance, patients with mood problems may require antidepressants and/or antipsychotics to stabilize their mood in addition to therapy. People with an anxiety disorder may also require anti-anxiety medications.

Please note that not all mental health conditions require medications. If your therapist thinks you need to see a psychiatrist, they will refer you. You can also decide to visit a psychiatrist by yourself if you deem it necessary. The doctor will prescribe medications for you if you need them.

The common medications prescribed to treat mental health disorders responsible for pathological lying include the following.

Antidepressants

Antidepressants increase the amount of mood-lifting hormones in your brain. These mood-lifting hormones include dopamine, norepinephrine, and serotonin. Selective serotonin reuptake inhibitors (SSRIs) and monoamine oxidase inhibitors are examples of common antidepressants.

Antipsychotics

Antipsychotics are a group of drugs used to treat a wide variety of mental health disorders. Doctors usually talk about first-generation and second-generation antipsychotics as treatment options for patients struggling with constant lying. First-generation antipsychotics have serious side effects. Second-generation antipsychotics, which are newer in the market, have only mild side effects.

Mood Stabilizers

Examples of mood stabilizers prescribed for people who lie compulsively include carbamazepine, lithium, and valproic acid. The exact mood stabilizer you need depends on the underlying mental health disorder. However, they are generally used in treating cyclic mood disorders and mania.

Talk to your provider if you want more information about the available options for your treatment. They can collaborate with your therapist or counselor to find the right treatment option for you.

7

Honesty is the Best Policy

Honesty is indeed the best policy. No matter how deep you are in the web of compulsive lying, you can make a turnaround and enjoy the benefits of honest living. This chapter will show you all the positive ripple affects you will gain from being more honest in your daily living.

Honestly Rebuilds Damaged Relationships

Honesty shows that you are treating your partner with dignity. It also breeds positivity, promotes communication, and reduces stress for both you and your partner. Quitting your lying habits will set your relationship up for success.

Little ways to practice honesty in your relationships include the following:

- Be open about your feelings and thoughts.
- Fulfill your promises. Do not promise anything you won't be able to do.
- Be consistent. Don't keep changing your mind on every issue.
- Say the truth regardless of the consequences. Don't protect yourself with a lie.
- Be a reliable person.

Must I Say Everything?

Honesty does not mean you have to be an open book to everybody. You can be an honest person and still maintain some privacy, even in your romantic relationship. You should, however, be honest about areas of your life that you are keeping private. Do not pretend that it is not a private matter or that you are being completely open.

For instance, if a friend confides in you about a personal issue, you should keep that information private. You are not under any obligation to tell your partner about the issue because you're practicing honesty. That would mean betraying your friend and being dishonest with them.

Here is another example. You may not want your colleagues at work to know about your pregnancy in the first few weeks. In that case, you are keeping the information about your pregnancy private. You are not keeping a secret or being dishonest.

That means honest living does not take away your right to withhold information. However, whenever you feel like withholding any piece of information, evaluate if that desire is coming from the need to keep the information private or to keep it a secret. That's where to draw the line between honesty and dishonesty.

I remember what happened between a couple that I once coached. The wife had a lying problem and was making efforts to become a better person. She felt the way to go about it was to tell her husband every single thought that crossed her mind. She felt she had to give him every little detail about everything.

While the lady felt she was improving, her husband concluded that it was all pretense. He felt she was just being overly dramatic to convince him that she was a changed person. Of course, it didn't end well. She soon lost motivation because her husband was never impressed by her efforts. She relapsed and blamed her husband for not being supportive.

I helped her see where she made a mistake and gave her the tip I shared above. She began to practice separating secrecy from privacy in filtering information. It helped her improve and her husband soon began to appreciate her efforts. She eventually reaped the benefits of honesty in her relationship.

On the Flip Side

There are lots of goodies on the flip side of dishonesty. Dishonesty will bring you distrust, strained relationships, and social disconnections. Honesty, on the other hand, will make you more trustworthy, build up your relationships, and help you build more social connections.

When Jack started addressing his lying problems, Alvine said she felt more loved and respected. She did not only trust Jack more, but she also said his honesty set a pattern for her and challenged her to become more honest herself. Such is the power of honest living.

According to the relationship expert, Rachael Pace, here are some benefits of honesty in a relationship:

A Trusting Partner

Trust is a very powerful tool in relationships. A trusting partner is always a better lover. When you become more honest with your partner, they will trust you more. Moreover, trusting partners are less likely to recall the mistakes of their partners or negative experiences in the relationship (Pace, 2021). Trust is, therefore, like a soothing balm that erases the pain of past lies and dishonesty.

Moreover, trust makes people feel safe in their relationships. Your partner will have a clearer headspace when they trust you.

Stronger Connection

Communication flows more freely when you have no skeletons to hide. That, in turn, helps your partner to build a stronger connection with you. Moreover, you will be able to resolve conflicts faster when there is a free flow of communication. You will have fewer instances where things go out of hand. All of these factors would help strengthen your connection.

Further, studies show that better communication helps couples to engage more positively. That would make your partner feel more satisfied and supported in the relationship.

Less Stress

Your partner will go through less stress when they don't have to wonder if you're being honest with them. If they can't take you for your word, there will always be questions on their mind. They would wonder if you were where you say you are. They'll think about who you're with or what you do on your phone when they are away, and so on. Living with these constant thoughts and questions in the mind is very stressful.

The constant thing I hear from the partners of those who lie compulsively is that the relationship is stressful. They say the constant worries and questions make them feel anxious and insecure. However, all of these come to an end when the lying partner starts being more honest.

Respect

I cannot overemphasize how honesty would make your partner feel respected. Telling them the truth shows that you respect their feelings and hold them in high esteem. Respecting their feelings in this way would boost their self-esteem, and they will reciprocate the respect.

One of my clients said nobody ever disrespected them the way their partner had done. They were not talking about nagging, yelling, or any such thing. Instead, they considered the constant lies, deceptions, and secrecy as the worst form of disrespect they ever experienced.

Life Satisfaction and Comfortability

Research shows that honesty means being vulnerable, and it gives your partner a sense of joy and reliability. These feelings make people exercise better self-control and feel more satisfied in life.

Being vulnerable to your partners also makes them more comfortable both in the relationship and generally in life. Experts even say that relationships are less boring when the partners feel secure and comfortable.

Mental Health

Did you know that partners who experience constant lies question whether they are truly worthy of love? Constant lies mess with the recipient's mental health and self-love. They may feel a lot of confusion, experience self-image issues, or become overly anxious about abandonment, among several other mental health disturbances.

Physical Health

Your brain experiences a cortisol surge within 10 minutes after stressful situations. The same thing happens to your partners each time they find out you lied to them or worry about whether you are lying to them. The brain overworks itself because of the cortisol surge and may cause other health issues, including:

- digestive problems

- chronic depression
- anxiety disorders
- lower immunity

No Guessing Games

There is nothing as frustrating in a relationship as playing guessing games. Nobody likes to feel like they need to read your mind. Nobody likes it when they have to drop subtle hints rather than say what's on their minds upfront. Sadly, that is what happens when one partner is dishonest.

When you start practicing more honesty in your relationship, your partner will not have to play guessing games with you. They will feel more comfortable discussing their wants, feelings, needs, and desires with you. They will also understand you better and know how to better relate with you when guessing games are off the table.

Many Personal Rewards

It may seem like only your partner or the vital relationships in your life will benefit from your honesty, but that is not true. There are many personal rewards for an honest living. They cut across your physical, mental, and emotional well-being. Here are some of the benefits you will get when you choose to adopt a life of honesty.

People Trust You More

The easiest way to ruin trust is to be repeatedly dishonest. Constant lies will damage your reputation and people will see you as a person who is not trustworthy. Such a bad reputation can cost you relationships and even future opportunities.

What would happen if you tell your spouse that you have to work late in the office? How would your colleagues respond if they heard that you called in late? All of these things matter. It affects how people relate to you and what they tell others about you.

I once had an online coaching client from another country. He felt like he was walking on eggshells around every vital relationship in his life. He had to answer one thousand and one questions from his wife whenever he was going on a business trip. His HR manager would also ask endless questions whenever he called in sick. Thankfully, he knew the source of the problems.

This client admitted that he had been a dishonest person. His family, workplace colleagues, and friends had caught him lying several times, so nobody trusted him. I coached him to become a more honest person and that was the game changer in his life. People began to trust him more and he didn't have to walk on eggshells anymore.

Less Work

It takes lots of energy to keep up with lies. You would have to maintain old lies by fabricating new lies. You would also have to work hard to cover both the old and new lies. Compulsive liars spend a lot of effort and time keeping a record of their many lies and coining creative words to hide their lies.

Honesty, on the other hand, requires less work. It allows you to divert your energy into more productive and positive activities.

Peace of Mind

Less stress and peace of mind are top among the hallmarks of honest living. Keeping up with lies, pretending, and walking on eggshells are a few of the stressful consequences of dishonesty. There is indeed no peace of mind for anyone who lies constantly. Quitting that habit will give you more peace and relieve you of unnecessary stress.

Chris, a client I coached last year, described the feeling as a breath of fresh air. He said he never knew life could be so peaceful and stress-free. That is what you stand to gain when you also embrace a life of honesty.

Better Health

Your health will improve when you eliminate stress from your daily living. Medical experts have linked chronic stress to stroke, heart issues, hypertension, and cancers. They also say chronic stress can increase the chances of premature death.

If stress from dishonesty can cause all of these health problems, then embracing a lifestyle of honesty will improve your health. The American Psychological Association published a study where researchers observed that people generally experience a health boost when they stop lying (Kelly et. al, 2012).

Please note that honesty does not replace the need for a healthy diet, rest, and exercise. However, a guiltless and clear conscience will help improve your health and make you a happier person.

More Confidence

Compulsive liars lack confidence because they have a lot to hide. They are often not sure if what they will say next will expose their lies and secrets. They have to pretend a lot and be on guard at all times. Their confidence is in who they pretend to be and not in their true identity. You may have experienced this if you used to lie compulsively.

An honest living will restore and boost your confidence. You can confidently say the truth without fear that it may expose one of your past lies. You can be yourself without any concerns about a falsified image you have presented to people.

You Attract Honest People

An adage says, "Birds of a feather flock together." That adage is so true when it comes to honest living. In life, you will always attract your kind. You will attract honest people when you are honest yourself. On the other hand, you will attract dishonest people if you are dishonest.

Those searching for committed friendships and relationships need to take honesty seriously. Otherwise, they will only attract dishonest people into their lives and hurt themselves in the process.

That does not mean that you can never fall prey to a toxic person if you are honest. It does, however, mean that you have fewer chances of attracting such people and more chances of attracting honest people.

Self-Reflection

I didn't realize that self-reflection could be a benefit of honesty until I had a review session with my star client, Jack. One of the tips I gave him was to be honest with himself. I shared the same tip in chapter 5 of this book.

During one of my review sessions with Jack, he said that the tip did more than help him to be honest. He said being honest with himself also allowed him to do a lot of self-reflection. He was compelled to reflect often on his feelings, thoughts, and intention. Jack said he was now more in tune with himself because he practiced that tip.

Who knows what honest living will do for you too? Being honest with yourself may be the push you need to do lots of self-reflection too. Like Jack, you may become more in tune with your thoughts, emotions, and intentions as you practice being honest with yourself.

Freedom

Constantly lying to people cages you in a constant state of guilt and shame. You may develop a coping mechanism for these feelings, but only honest living can offer you true freedom.

Jack experienced another kind of freedom when he became a more honest person. He had asked a few friends to corroborate his lies on a few occasions. He felt indebted to these friends, and that was affecting his conscience. What's more, he had to be careful around those friends because they had the power to expose him.

Honesty broke Jack free from the bondage of his lies. His conscience was free and he could sleep well every night. He was also no longer indebted to any friend. You can enjoy the same measure of freedom when you start practicing honesty.

Your Opinions Would Count

People generally find it hard to respect the opinion of a dishonest person. They will hardly ask for your opinion when they suspect that you won't be honest with them. Conversely, they will not only ask for your opinion when they trust you, but they will also respect it. Your honest opinions may sometimes hurt their feelings, but they will appreciate them in the long run.

For instance, your partner may stop asking you if their outfit has matching colors when they know you won't tell the truth. They will rather ask someone who will tell them the candid truth to avoid public embarrassment.

Telling them the truth may seem hurtful, but don't hide it from them. Just make sure you are tactful in your approach, and they will appreciate your honesty and respect your opinions. Further, being honest in minor issues like their choice of outfit sends a signal to your significant other that they can count on your opinion in significant situations, like business deals and major life decisions.

Positive Atmosphere

Lying habits create a toxic environment in relationships. For instance, you may realize that your significant other picks fights with you easily and stays angry for long after quarrels. You may also notice that your boss queries almost everything you do and picks on every little mistake you make. All of these reactions may be because they are frustrated about something else: your lying habits.

The atmosphere would become more positive when you become a more honest person. You will have less toxicity around you, and you would start attracting more positive things into your life. Your positive experience will, in turn, make you more positive about the future and life in general.

Honesty is the best policy by all standards. Your relationships will be better for it. Everyone around you will also benefit from your honesty. Chief of all, you will also gain a lot from becoming a more honest person. It may take a lot of effort, but it's worth it in the end.

8

Worth it in the End

The transformation process from being a compulsive liar to becoming an honest person is difficult, but it is possible and worth the effort. In my professional practice, I have observed that the results vary from person to person. Some of my clients started seeing results after a few sessions. Some clients, on the other hand, only start seeing significant results after months of coaching and therapy.

I always remind the clients that experience immediate improvements that therapy is not a quick fix. I tell them that we still need to keep digging until we discover the underlying cause of their lying behaviors. Fixing the underlying issue is the road to a more honest, satisfying, and fulfilling life.

I have recorded a high rate of success with clients using this approach. All of these success stories have something in common. The clients were willing and cooperative throughout the therapy process. They also refused to give up when they experienced setbacks.

Ebb and Flow

The difficulty with overcoming compulsive lying, just as with any other behavioral disorder, is the need to consistently resist temptations. You may successfully stop lying for a week or two and slip back into the behavior. Over time, it may feel like you are running in cycles, and you may start becoming frustrated.

Have you heard about ebb and flow before? It refers to a rhythmical pattern of growth and decline. To be honest, that is the reality about overcoming compulsive lying. You cannot become perfect overnight, so you must keep exerting efforts daily.

Are You Willing?

Most compulsive liars do not see the reason why they should seek treatment or commit to a process of change. Most compulsive liars only seek help because a court order directed them to do so. Others seek help when their lying behavior has landed them in serious trouble, such as divorce, bankruptcy, or career setbacks.

The problem here is that lasting change is only possible when a person willingly seeks help. The person who is compelled by the court or a pressing life situation will soon lose motivation. They are likely to back out of the process somewhere along the line. They may hang on for a few months, but they will eventually back out if there is no personal desire for change.

Almost every pathological liar that genuinely desires change will require long-term therapy. That would mean about one to three therapy sessions weekly for several months or even years. Are you willing to commit to a long-term process if that's what you need? It may seem difficult, but I promise you that it's worth it in the end.

Lying Feels Good Until...

Your lying behavior may hurt you and your relationships in many ways, but it also helps you in some ways. You probably find it easier to lie or feel better when you lie. It is your default behavior, so it is normal to slip back into it whenever you lose guard.

You only start feeling bad after the moment has passed. Feelings of shame and inadequacy may set in. You may feel horrible and helpless because it seems you can't control the habit.

Other secondary issues may come up too. For instance, the truth may come out, the people you love may feel hurt, or you may experience turbulence in your relationship. All of these can make you even more frustrated.

How about the many times you have promised your loved one that you will change? You may become unhappy because you broke your promise to them again.

Do not accommodate these negative feelings. They will discourage you in the long run and make you worse off. I know several people who resigned to fate after their "failed attempts." Those that eventually succeeded in their quest for honest living were relentless. They refused to give up even when it seemed they would never succeed.

Habits Are Hard to Break

The benefits you get from lying are not the only reason why you may experience an ebb and flow in your transformation process. Remember that lying has been a part of your life for a long time. It has become a habit, so it won't go away easily.

That means you can lie mindlessly without even thinking about it. In that case, you didn't lie because of any immediate benefit. It was just a default response because of how you have trained your kind over the years. Lying has become second nature because you used to lie so frequently.

It does not matter how many times you have vowed to change; your default habits will get the best of you once in a while. Don't allow these incidents to dissuade you. It does not mean your efforts are not productive. It just means you need to keep pushing until you break the bad habit.

Life Feels Different

This is yet another reason why it seems you're running around in circles. For compulsive liars, lying is an identity. It's who you have become over time, so your life feels different when lying is no longer a part of it.

I have coached clients who wondered what their lives would look like without lying. Some of them have built a false persona for themselves over the years. What would become of their lives when they do away with the false persona and start being their real selves? That's another reason why people relapse, and you might experience it too.

I'll be frank with you. It is normal if you find it hard to imagine what your life would look or feel like when you become an honest person. It is normal to slip back into lying once in a while because it's hard to embrace your new personality. Don't give up when these things happen. With time, you will get used to honest living.

The Dilemma

Most people who have attempted to change a bad habit will tell you they had a dilemma somewhere along the line. They were scared of their bad habit, but they were also scared of stopping it. For instance, while you strongly desire to change, you may still find it difficult to come to terms with the consequences of honesty.

The dilemma can put you in a fix and make the struggle worse. It may seem like your efforts are futile because you keep slipping, but that's not true. Brace up to the challenge and keep putting in the effort. Remember that the reasons why you want to quit lying are still valid. I know it's a lot of work, but it will pay off in the end.

Keep Getting Back on Track

I tell my clients that the smoothest pathway to overcoming their struggles with pathological lying is preventing a relapse. However, a relapse should not end your change process. No matter how many times you fall, make sure you keep rising.

Taking a cue from 12 Keys Rehab, here are some vital steps you should take whenever a relapse occurs (12 Keys Rehab, 2016).

Accept Responsibility

It will certainly take daily practice to do this, but try to accept responsibility as soon as a relapse occurs. Remember that it's up to you and no one else to adjust your lifestyle. No matter what caused your relapse, accept responsibility for slipping. Don't try to shift the blame to others or play the victim.

Accepting that you made a mistake and still need help is your first step to receiving help. Practicing this level of self-accountability will help you sustain a high level of motivation despite your relapse.

Take Immediate Action

Don't stay in your mess. Take immediate steps to pick up your journey toward honest living again. Remember why you started seeking a turnaround in the first place. It will give you the motivation and strength to continue your turnaround process.

The longer it takes you to act, the more difficult it will become. Picking up your winning strategies will start seeming like hard work, and you will find it easier to continue in your old habits.

Invariably, waiting too long to take action will make you susceptible to several other mistakes after the initial slip. Then, your old lying habit will start working its way into your life again.

Ask for Support

You need a strong support network to overcome compulsive lying. I have realized that how much support you get after each relapse will determine how quickly and how well you'll get back on track. It will also help prevent future relapses during vulnerable moments.

Moreover, research shows that those who lack adequate support often quit their turnaround process after a relapse. As such, ensure to reach out to your partner, friends, family, or other people in your support circle. Open up to them about the relapse and let them motivate you to keep keeping on.

Work on Your Mind

Everything starts from the mind. You will succeed if your mind can conceive success, but you will fail if your mind conceives failure. That's why you must be intentional about what's going on in your mind. Ensure to direct your mind's attention away from the slip and refocus it on your turnaround process.

Don't judge yourself or beat yourself up for the mistake. Stay positive and focus on future opportunities to make better choices. Keep affirming to yourself that you are still committed to the turnaround process and will give it your best shot.

Further, your mind may feel too tired to go back to square one. Don't see it that way, otherwise, you will be tempted to skip vital steps. Keep reminding yourself that you are no longer where you used to be. You are now passionate about becoming a better person and you are working toward it.

Continue Therapy

Don't conclude that therapy is not working and quit because you had a slip. Also, don't assume that your support system can take the place of professional help. There is no valid replacement for the professional knowledge, expert care, and personalized strategy that therapists and behavioral specialists offer. They will help you deal with your mistake, get back to your turnaround strategies, and offer insight on how to prevent future slips.

Redesign Your Plan

I mentioned earlier that a slip does not mean all your efforts failed. It, however, means there may be a need to redesign your plan. Tie any loose ends and close up any cracks that may have contributed to the relapse.

I tell clients that once we can identify why they slipped, we can redesign their plan to address the trigger. As such, visit your therapist and analyze the slip. Talk about the situation that led to it, and see how you can improve your current plan to prevent further occurrences.

You may conclude that you need to add some new strategies or consider another type of therapy. Your therapist may also refer you to a mental health expert for medical treatment. Whatever the case may be, the goal is to have a stronger and more formidable plan with which you can face future challenges and overcome them.

Repair Broken Relationships

Did you hurt, betray, or disappoint anyone when you slipped and lied again? You should take active steps to mend the relationship. Don't stop at getting back to your turnaround process. Seek forgiveness from those you hurt and put in the effort to repair the broken relationship.

Explain what happened and let them know that you are still taking steps to become a better person. Assure them that you will do your very best not to hurt them or undermine your relationship with them again.

Consider doing the following things as you attempt to repair broken relationships after your relapse.

● Write them a letter or have a one-on-one discussion to own up to the lie, tell them you feel bad about it, and apologize for hurting them.

• Give them quality time and attention if they want to talk about how they feel about your actions. Allow them to vent and say everything on their minds.

• Invite them to attend therapy sessions with you if they are close enough. That will help them understand how much effort you're making, motivate them not to give up on you, and show them better ways to support you in the journey. Moreover, it will make your bond stronger and go a long way in helping repair the damage in your relationship.

Expect Discomfort

Nobody likes to make mistakes, especially when they are trying hard not to. Making mistakes can stir up feelings of regret, shame, guilt, frustration, and other painful emotions. These feelings will pass with time, so don't dwell on them. I know that it's not an easy process, but expect these feelings and quickly move on from them when they come.

The common discomforts my clients report experiencing after a slip include:

• low self-esteem
• fatigue and demotivation
• feeling like people are judging you
• self-doubt
• irritation
• aggression
• emotional distress

Watch out for them and let them pass. However, speak with a professional if any of these feelings linger beyond a few days after your slip.

Learn Your Lessons

What's the point if you learned nothing from your mistakes? The lessons you learn from the slip will empower you to exercise better control over the behavior in the future. As such, make sure to review the situation with your therapist and support network to reflect on the lessons you learned from the mistake.

You Need a Support System

Any person seeking to break a stubborn habit, like pathological lying, needs a strong support system for after and better outcomes. As such, I recommend that you get your partner, family, and close friends involved in your change process. You need people to lean on when the going gets tough.

Many people in your life are willing to support you in your quest for a more honest living. However, many of them don't know how to go about it. Since you know your needs more than anyone else, you should take the lead and advocate for their support in clear terms.

Here is what I teach my clients to do to build a strong support system for themselves.

Ask For Their Support

Many people complain that nobody was there for them in their time of need. The first question I ask when clients say that is, "Did you ask them for help?" People are not likely to offer support if they don't know you need it.

They may know about your lying habits, but you need to tell them about the efforts you're making. Let them know what you are doing to improve and ask for their support through the process.

Accept Help

Appreciate people that offer support and accept their help. It is normal for people to suggest one or two tips because they care about you. Accepting help does not mean that you must do everything they suggest. However, it means you must admit that they have good intentions. It also means you should appreciate them and collaborate with them.

Further, tell them what you are doing and let them hold you accountable. Don't think they are overbearing when they try to keep you on track. Use all the help you can get.

A Shoulder to Lean On

Many times, what you need is a shoulder to lean on. You need people who will make time for you and give you listening ears. Recognize the people who are willing to offer you their shoulders and lean on them. Talk to them about your frustrations, share your pains with them, and let them motivate you to keep pushing.

Be Clear

People cannot read your mind, so be clear about what you need from them. Also, let them know what you don't need. Communicate this tactfully so that it won't seem like you're pushing them away.

I have a standard approach I recommend for my clients. You can use this approach to be clear about your needs without hurting the feelings of those who desire to help you.

Start by appreciating them for offering you help. Mention the specific thing they are doing or attempting to do. Go on to tell them what you would prefer or like them to do instead. Finish up by asking if that's something they would be willing to do for you.

Assume that you lied at work and decided to open up to your partner about the slip. As soon as you told them, they started telling you how you should have handled the situation. You can tell them, "Thank you so much for your comments, but what I need right now is the encouragement to keep trying. Can you please do that for me?"

I know that people can be a handful sometimes. Just make sure you set healthy boundaries and appreciate everything they do to help you.

A Walking Example

Anyone who can turn a new leaf and quit lying compulsively is a star. It is no small achievement at all. As such, you should celebrate your little wins. Also, use your experience to encourage and help others when you have improved.

Becoming a walking example helps you sustain the motivation to keep going. There are several ways to do that, but I often recommend the following to my clients.

Participate in Community Groups for Pathological Liars

Being part of a community support group offers many benefits. You will be an inspiration to members of the group who are just starting their turnaround journey. You will also draw inspiration from others in the group. Everyone will have access to social support and share insight on coping skills and improvement tips that work.

People have friends and family who can support them. However, they may not always understand the struggles of compulsive lying. You have been there, so you understand the struggle and can empathize better. You can also offer practicable tips from your personal experiences.

Enhancing the motivation of others will boost your psychological and emotional well-being. Moreover, helping others replicate your victory makes your efforts to seek a turnaround even more worthwhile. Your success will become more fulfilling as you offer help to others who want to achieve the same results as you.

I remember when I encouraged Jack to find a support group for pathological liars in his community. He was initially hesitant but later decided to give it a try. The sessions were so fulfilling that Jack felt he finally found his life purpose. Now, he oversees a network of social support groups for compulsive liars. Jack has become a symbol of hope for every pathological liar he meets.

A Note for First-Timers

It is normal to be anxious as you prepare for your first support group meeting. Don't hesitate to go with a friend or family member if that will make you more comfortable. Also, keep the following things in mind.

• Group members may open up about difficult experiences and intricate life details during the group session. Please, respect their confidentiality and never talk about it outside the group.

• You don't have to say anything. You can keep quiet and observe throughout the meeting. There is no pressure whatsoever. Share only what you're comfortable talking about if you choose to talk. You can open up and share more details when you know the group members better and become more comfortable with them.

● Don't hesitate to ask questions about the things you don't understand. That includes questions about processes within the group and the roles of members, among other things. Clear understanding helps you feel more connected in the group and enhances effective participation.

● Remember that you are not just there to give. You are also there to learn from the experiences of your peers.

Write About Your Journey

A few of my clients are writing their soon-to-be-published memoirs. Telling their stories through writing gives a better perspective on their journeys so far and helps them appreciate how far they have come. Moreover, their stories are very inspiring. They get inspired by their own stories while writing and get to inspire others too after publishing the memoir.

What if you are not the storytelling type of person? There are professional story writers that can help you write your story. They will chat with you, listen to your story, and ask you questions to help them write your story exactly the way it is.

Another option is to journal your turnaround process and inspire people with it. I love this option because it's right at the moment. All you need is a pen and a pad. You may even use your smartphone if carrying a pen and pad around will be too burdensome for you.

Note your successes and failures in the journal. Identify the motivations or strategies that helped you succeed and the triggers that led to failures. Write down your thoughts immediately after each episode and what you learned.

Share Your Story With a Public Audience

You can inspire several people by sharing your story with a public audience. Those struggling with compulsive lying will learn from your experience. Some people who never saw the need to seek a turnaround will be challenged to work toward leading a more honest life.

Moreover, others in the audience who have different behavioral conditions will also be inspired by your story. They would realize that their case is neither special nor hopeless. Further, your story may help some people see that therapy works and subsequently seek professional help.

AFTERWORD

Change is the most powerful force in life, and there's nothing you can do to stop change. If you try to resist change, life will become difficult. That's often the case with pathological liars who resist change and continue in their lying habits.

The consequences of lying force many compulsive liars to reconsider their lying habits. However, that kind of crisis-induced change doesn't last long; the motivation would wane after a while. You can only achieve lasting change when you choose to put in the effort. That is what this book has been all about.

You need three things to kickstart your process of turnaround from compulsive lying.

● Insight: Knowing that you have a problem with lying and need to fix it.

● Willingness: The desire to take steps towards quitting your lying behavior.

● Commitment: Refusal to give up no matter how tough the process is or how long it takes.

Change is indeed possible, but you must make it happen.

Compulsive Lying: Behavior or Habit?

Psychologists have yet to identify compulsive or pathological lying as a mental health disorder. Conversely, they recognize it as a bad habit and a behavioral disorder.

There is, however, a slight difference between behaviors and habits. A behavior is something you do frequently due to an internal or external influence. People around you can observe your behavior. Habits, on the other hand, are automated actions. They are things you do repeatedly until they begin to happen through your subconscious drive.

Behaviors require conscious thoughts or intention, but habits require neither. Habits are, therefore, more difficult to treat than behaviors. Lying has become a habit for some people, but thankfully, lying habits can be fixed.

Explore the Underlying Cause

It is essential to explore the underlying cause of your lying problems. That is where the journey of transformation truly begins. You must dig until you understand why you lie a lot. That understanding will guide you and your therapist on the right treatment strategy. Moreover, you are more likely to succeed in your quest for change when you address the issue from its roots.

Think about a mighty tree that has grown so big, and you want to get rid of it. You can cut the tree, leave its stump, and everything will seem alright. However, unless you uproot it, it will eventually sprout again someday. That is how to view compulsive lying and other behavioral disorders. Unless you address the root cause, any change you see is only temporary.

Three Key Players

There are three key players in your change process if you want to become more honest. You are the first key player because everything lies in your hands. Ultimately, only you have the power to change your life. Others may guide and/or support you through the process, but you must take responsibility for your transformation.

Your support system is the second key player in your turnaround process. You need your significant other, friends, and family to rally around you as you take bold steps to become more honest. Their motivation, emotional support, and accountability system will amplify your efforts.

The third key player is your therapist. You may try self-help with the tips in this book, but don't hesitate to see a therapist if you need professional help. Most compulsive liars would need professional help somewhere along the line. Cooperate with your therapist to get the best possible outcome from the process.

A Fourth Key Player

Pathological lying may occur secondary to a mental health disorder. If that is the case, you would need a fourth key player: a mental health specialist. Change is unlikely if you ignore the underlying mental health challenge in your attempts to stop lying compulsively.

Stay Motivated

You have read about how lying affects you and those you are lying to, so we don't have to go over them again. We have also talked about all the reasons why you should quit compulsive lying. Identify which ones resonate with you the most. Pinpoint your strong reasons for wanting change, and keep them at the center of your heart.

Let those reasons keep fueling your motivation no matter how tough the journey gets. Success is sure if your motivation remains intact. Further, remember that every behavior is learned. That means you can unlearn them too. It may take time, but you will eventually unlearn your lying behavior.

Live in the Moment

Forget about the past and move on from it. I know you have made many mistakes, and you regret them. Nevertheless, don't keep reliving those moments. Focus on rebuilding whatever is left of your damaged relationships and becoming a better person.

Don't worry about the future either. Don't visualize future slips into lying or negative consequences of honesty. Just live in the moment and keep winning. Celebrate your little wins and remain hopeful that things will keep getting better. And if you fall, rise again.

You will win! The world awaits your success story.

REFERENCES

Alvarez, S. (2017, October 26). What Is Lying By Omission And How Does It Harm Relationships? A Conscious Rethink. https://www.aconsciousrethink.com/6477/lie-of-omission/

Barkley, S. (2022, August 11). Compulsive Liar vs. Pathological Liar: Traits, Mental Health, and More. Psych Central. https://psychcentral.com/blog/deliberately-untruthful-normal-vs-abnormal-lying

Barzacchini, M. (2022, June 7). Exaggeration: Lying or Not? – #MTtalk Twitter chat Roundup. Mind Tools. https://www.mindtools.com/blog/exaggeration-lying-or-not/

Bates-Duford, T. (2019, January 18). Harmful Family Lies, Secrets, and Legacies. Psych Central. https://psychcentral.com/blog/relationship-corner/2019/01/harmful-family-lies-secrets-and-legacies

Better Help Editorial Team. (2022, November 29). How To Recognize A Pathological Liar. Betterhelp. https://www.betterhelp.com/advice/general/how-to-recognize-pathological-lying/

Bhattacharjee, Y. (2017, May 18). Why We Lie: The Science Behind Our Deceptive Ways. Magazine. https://www.nationalgeographic.com/magazine/article/lying-hoax-false-fibs-science

Buddy, T. (2021, September 1). How to Find a Support Group Meeting Near You. Verywell Mind. https://www.verywellmind.com/find-a-support-group-meeting-near-you-69433

Burton, N. (2019, September 24). The Philosophy of Lying. Neel Burton Personal Website and Blog. https://neelburton.com/2019/09/24/the-philosophy-of-lying/

Carson, T. L. (2006). The Definition of Lying. Noûs, 40(2), 284–306. https://www.jstor.org/stable/3506133

Carucci, A. (2022, September 26). Can Someone Really Change Their Behaviors, Traits, and Habits? Psychcentral.com. https://psychcentral.com/blog/can-people-really-change

Cherry, K. (2019, October 29). How to Tell if Someone is Lying.? Verywell Mind. https://www.verywellmind.com/how-to-tell-if-someone-is-lying-2795917

Compulsive Liar Disorder Treatment | Stop Habitual or Pathological Lying. (n.d.). Bayside Psychotherapy. https://www.baysidepsychotherapy.com.au/compulsive-lying-therapy/

Compulsive Lying. (2018, August 5). GoodTherapy Blog. https://www.goodtherapy.org/blog/psychpedia/compulsive-lying

Curtis, D. A., & Hart, C. L. (2020, December 11). Pathological Lying: Theoretical and Empirical Support for a Diagnostic Entity. Psychiatric Research and Clinical Practice, 2(2). https://doi.org/10.1176/appi.prcp.20190046

Davies, J. (2022, May 15). 8 Psychological Effects of Being Lied to (and Why People Lie). Learning Mind.https://www.learning-mind.com/psychological-effects-of-being-lied-to/

Dishner, J. (2014, October 9). 7 Ways to Get The Emotional Support You Need From Friends. Hellalife. https://www.hellalife.com/blog/community/emotional-support/

Doheny, K. (2016, February 16). The Truth Behind Pathological and Compulsive Liars. EverydayHealth. https://www.everydayhealth.com/emotional-health/truth-behind-pathological-compulsive-liars/

Drummond, R. (2015). 10 Top Signs That Someone is Lying. Forensics Colleges. https://www.forensicscolleges.com/blog/resources/10-signs-someone-is-lying

8 Ways Lying Is Poisonous To Relationships. (2016, June 23). A Conscious Rethink. https://www.aconsciousrethink.com/3711/8-ways-lying-poisonous-relationships

Edwards, V. V. (2013, February 12). Human Lie Detection and Body Language 101: Your Guide to Reading People's Nonverbal Behavior. Goodreads. https://www.goodreads.com/book/show/17398207-human-lie-detection-and-body-language-101

Ekman, P. (2018, September 25). Why Do People Lie: 9 Motives for Telling Lies. Paul Ekman Group. https://www.paulekman.com/blog/why-do-people-lie-motives/

Enorcena Wiki. (2021, June 15). The 15 types of lies (and their characteristics). Enorcena. https://enorcerna.com/wiki/psychology/the-15-types-of-lies-and-their-characteristics/

Field, B. (2021, May 17). Is it Ever Okay to Lie? Verywell Mind. https://www.verywellmind.com/is-it-ever-okay-to-lie-5118228

Gonsalves, K. (2022, August 22). Why Honesty In a Relationship is Non-Negotiable & 7 Rules to Follow. Mindbodygreen. https://www.mindbodygreen.com/articles/why-honesty-in-a-relationship-is-so-important

Greenberg, E. (2020, August 1). Why Narcissists Twist The Truth: Logical Explanation. Mind Journal. https://themindsjournal.com/why-narcissists-twist-the-truth/

Harris, S. (2013). Lying. (Google Ebook). Four Elephants Press. https://books.google.com.jm/books?id=aVz_BgAAQBAJ&printsec=frontcover&dq=the+effects+of+lying&hl=en&sa=X

Holmes, T. (n.d.). How to Make Up After Telling a Lie. EHow UK. Retrieved December 17, 2022, from https://www.ehow.co.uk/12106650/how-to-make-up-after-telling-a-lie

Hurd, S. (2019, November 16). The Illusion of Truth and How Liars & Manipulators Are Using It to Trick You. Learning Mind. https://www.learning-mind.com/the-illusion-of-truth-manipulation/

Iliades, C. (2010, July 14). The Truth About Lies. EverydayHealth. https://www.everydayhealth.com/longevity/truth-about-lies-and-longevity.aspx

Is omission the same as lying? (2021, April 12). Short Facts. https://short-facts.com/is-omission-the-same-as-lying/

Keller, R. R. (2016, April 25). The Problem With Lying To Your Friends And Family. The Odyssey Online. https://www.theodysseyonline.com/problem-lying-friends-family

Kumar, K., & Radhakrishnan, R. (2022, December 14). What Is the Difference Between a Pathological Liar and a Compulsive Liar? MedicineNet. https://www.medicinenet.com/pathological_liar_vs_a_compulsive_liar/article.htm

Lancer, D. (2018, January 31). How Secrets and Lies Destroy Relationships. Psychology Today. https://www.psychologytoday.com/us/blog/toxic-relationships/201801/how-secrets-and-lies-destroy-relationships

Larissa. (2012, July 2). Withholding the Truth vs. Lying. Larisa Explains It All. http://www.larissaexplainsitall.com/2012/07/withholding-truth-vs-lying.html

Lebow, H. I. (2022, September 15). How to Spot a Pathological Liar: Signs, Causes, and How to Deal. Psych Central. https://psychcentral.com/health/signs-pathological-liar

Longstaff, S., & Saunders, A. (2005, July 20). The Philosophy of Lying [Radio Broadcast]. ABC Radio National. https://www.abc.net.au/radionational/programs/philosopherszone/the-philosophy-of-lying/3353848

Lying and Deception Destroys Trust. (2018). Truth About Deception. https://www.truthaboutdeception.com/lying-and-deception/pros-and-cons-of-lying/drawbacks/destroys-trust.html

Lying in the Workplace (and Why It Happens). (2020, June 9). Connected HR. https://connected-hr.com/lying-in-the-workplace-and-why-it-happens/

Mahon, J. E. (2015, December 25). The Definition of Lying and Deception (E. N. Zalta, Ed.). Stanford Encyclopedia of Philosophy; Metaphysics Research Lab, Stanford University. https://plato.stanford.edu/entries/lying-definition

Mahon, J. E. (2018, December 11). Classic Philosophical Approaches to Lying and Deception. The Oxford Handbook of Lying, 12–31. https://doi.org/10.1093/oxfordhb/9780198736578.013.2

Major, A. (n.d.). ask ammanda: My partner is a compulsive liar. Relate.org. https://www.relate.org.uk/get-help/my-partner-compulsive-liar

Marks, T. (2020, August 26). Pathological Lying Vs Normal Lying? How To Tell the Difference [Video file]. Youtube. https://youtu.be/zRm9i_YzTvI

Matsumoto, D., & Hwang, H. C. (2020). Clusters of Nonverbal Behavior Differentiate Truths And Lies About Future Malicious Intent in Checkpoint Screening Interviews. Psychiatry, Psychology and Law, 1–16. https://doi.org/10.1080/13218719.2020.1794999

Mazur, T. C. (2015, November 13). Lying. Santa Clara University. https://www.scu.edu/ethics/ethics-resources/ethical-decision-making/lying

McPhillips, K. (2019, September 30). The Fine Line That Separates Compulsive Liars From Over-Exaggerators. Well+Good. https://www.wellandgood.com/over-exaggeration/

Natarajan, H. (2022, December 12). 6 Different Types Of Liars And How To Deal With Them. STYLECRAZE. https://www.stylecraze.com/articles/types-of-liars/

Pace, R. (2022, April 13). Why Honesty in a Relationship Is So Important. Marriage.com. https://www.marriage.com/advice/relationship/honesty-in-a-relationship/

Pearson, P. (n.d.). Why We Lie, and How to Get Back to the Truth. Couples Institute. https://www.couplesinstitute.com/why-we-lie/

Power of Positivity. (2021, June 1). 10 Benefits of Honesty in a Relationship. Power of Positivity: Positive Thinking & Attitude. https://www.powerofpositivity.com/honesty-relationship-positive-benefits/

Preuter, S., Jaeger, B., & Stel, M. (2021, January 31). The Costs of Lying : Consequences of Telling Self-Centered and Other-Oriented Lies on the Self-Esteem and Affect of Liars. University of Twente. http://essay.utwente.nl/85697/

Quinn, D. (2022, October 27). What To Do After a Relapse: 9 Steps to Help You Get Back on Track and Sober. Sandstone Care. https://www.sandstonecare.com/blog/what-to-do-after-a-relapse-9-steps-to-help-you-get-back-on-track-and-sober/

Robb-Dover, K. (2021, April 12). Pathological Lying Can Occur with These Mental Disorders. FHE Health. https://fherehab.com/learning/pathological-lying-disorders

Saltz, G. (2011, March 24). How to Conquer Your Compulsions. Woman's Day. https://www.womansday.com/health-fitness/womens-health/how-to/a5583/how-to-conquer-your-compulsions-116339/

Sandford, K. (2023, January 5). 16 Things You Can Do to Change Your Life in 2023. Lifehack. https://www.lifehack.org/310325/10-things-change-your-life-forever

Santos-Longhurst, A., & Legg, T. J. (2018, August 27). Pathological Liar: How to Cope with Someone's Compulsive Lies. Healthline. https://www.healthline.com/health/pathological-liar#comparing-lies

Schocket, R. (2021, October 27). How Cheaters and Liars React to Being Called Out. BuzzFeed. https://www.buzzfeed.com/ryanschocket2/how-cheaters-liars-react-to-being-called-out

Schuder, K. (2022, November 2). Potential Treatments for Pathological Lying. LoveToKnow. https://www.lovetoknowhealth.com/well-being/treatment-for-compulsive-lying

Serota, K. B., & Levine, T. (2014, January 1). A Few Prolific Liars. ResearchGate. https://www.researchgate.net/publication/262262504_A_Few_Prolific_Liars

Share Your Story. (n.d.). SAMHSA. https://www.samhsa.gov/brss-tacs/recovery-support-tools/share-your-story

Smith, M., Robinson, L., & Segal, J. (2022, December 30) Obsessive-Compulsive Disorder. HelpGuide. https://www.helpguide.org/articles/anxiety/obssessive-compulsive-disorder-ocd.htm

Smith, R. R. (2010, February 21). To be or not to be: Is it lying to withhold information? The Times. https://www.thetimes.co.uk/article/to-be-or-not-to-be-is-it-lying-to-withhold-information-52lkrpfhwx9

Sullivan, B. (2020, January 5). The Truth About Lying and What It Does to the Body. Psychology Today. https://www.psychologytoday.com/us/blog/pleased-meet-me/202001/the-truth-about-lying-and-what-it-does-the-body

Talan, R. C. (2022, May 5). 5 Ways to Practice Honesty in Life. Inspiring Tips. https://inspiringtips.com/ways-to-practice-honesty-in-life/

Ten Tips for What to Do After Relapse Occurs - 12 Keys. (2016, March 8). 12 Keys Rehab. https://www.12keysrehab.com/10-tips-for-what-to-do-after-relapse-occurs/

WebMD Editorial Contributors. (2020, November 23). Signs of Lying. WebMD. https://www.webmd.com/mental-health/signs-lying

WebMD Editorial Contributors. (2021, October 25). What to Know About Pathological Liars. WebMD. https://www.webmd.com/mental-health/what-to-know-pathological-liars

Why it's so hard to change a behavior (& how DBT can help). (2016, August 10). Bay Area DBT & Couples Counseling Center. https://bayareadbtcc.com/hard-change-a-behavior/

Wikipedia editors. (2022, November 13). Schema Therapy. Wikipedia. https://en.wikipedia.org/wiki/Schema_therapy

Wiltermuth, S., Newman, D., & Raj, M. (2015, May 26). The Consequences of Dishonesty. Society for Personality and Social Psychology. https://spsp.org/news-center/character-context-blog/consequences-dishonesty

Zembaty, J. S. (1988). Plato's Republic and Greek Morality on Lying. Journal of the History of Philosophy, 26(4), 517–545. https://doi.org/10.1353/hph.1988.0079